THE
PROSPERITY
AND
DEPRESSION
DECADES

Hayden Twentieth Century Issues Series

THE BLACK MAN IN THE LAND OF EQUALITY
Thomas J. Ladenburg and William S. McFeely

THE PROSPERITY AND DEPRESSION DECADES
Thomas J. Ladenburg and Samuel Hugh Brockunier

THE PROSPERITY AND DEPRESSION DECADES

THOMAS J. LADENBURG
Educational Development Center
Formerly, Lee High School, New Haven

SAMUEL HUGH BROCKUNIER
Wesleyan University

HAYDEN BOOK COMPANY, INC., NEW YORK

Acknowledgments:

The authors wish to thank Stowell Symmes for his many helpful suggestions on the presentation of economic concepts in this book, and Muriel Ladenburg for untold hours of proof reading, typing and encouragement and consultation.

All copyrighted material from the New York Times is reprinted by permission of the New York Times Company.

Excerpts from "Johnson vs Poverty" are reprinted by permission of THE NEW REPUBLIC, © 1964, Harrison-Blaine of New Jersey.

Material from Otto Eckstein's Public Finance, 2nd ed., © 1967 is reprinted by permission of Prentice-Hall, Inc., Englewood Cliffs, New Jersey.

Excerpts from "Spending Into Trouble" originally appeared in the Saturday Evening Post issue, May 18, 1963. Copyright © 1963 by Dwight D. Eisenhower. Reprinted by permission of Doubleday & Company, Inc.

Preface

The colorful and dramatic history of the 1920's and 1930's is often told so as to leave obscure the significant economic issues of that period. Few students are ignorant about scar-faced Al Capone or prohibition, but far fewer understand the concept of farm parity or the income multiplier. While the history of the jazz era is undoubtedly interesting, an economic history can be both fascinating and instructive; a nation that understands its economic past is less likely to repeat its mistakes.

This book teaches the economic concepts indispensible to understanding the business cycle while encouraging that frame of mind which will guard against blind acceptance of conventional wisdoms. Parity, margin, the flow of goods, services, and payments, the investment multiplier, and deficit spending, are explained and analyzed. The student's interest in these concepts is aroused and sustained by setting them within the framework of the public controversies which have made them important tools for understanding. The student debates the causes of poverty and what government should do about it; are the poor responsible for their condition or is society? He argues the wisdom of following policies favorable to business interests; are these interests identical with the national interest?

Disagreement over issues of public policy usually reflects a fundamental difference in values; students have a chance to develop and test their own political philosophies by discussing the issues raised in this book. They can match their ideas against the notions of their classmates, the concepts of economics, and the facts of history. The task for this book, therefore, and for the teacher who accepts its challenge, is to present economic concepts in a manner which permits students to argue for those policies which represent meaningful alternatives in the decade ahead. The guiding assumptions of this work are that students are perfectly capable of making judgments on controversial issues, that learning increases when conclusions are arrived at rather than imposed, and that the job of the teachers (authors included) is nothing more or less than the encouragement of this inquiry in an atmosphere of mutual respect for free expression.

The major sections of the book coincide with three important decades and the issues they raise. During the 1920's belief in the benign power of Adam Smith's invention, the 'unseen hand,' was still an article of economic faith. The distribution of economic rewards was to be determined in the market place, not in the halls of government, and those who fared poorly were paying for some sin or shortcoming. Presidents Harding, Coolidge and Hoover followed conservative philosophies; they balanced the budget, lowered taxes, and reduced expenditures by vetoing those measures designed to help any but business interests. Since unprecedented prosperity followed, it is understandable that Americans affirmed their faith in conservative policies. Farmers, miners, textile workers, and other major groups did not participate in the prosperity, but it was assumed that a continuation of the policies of the twenties would abolish poverty during the thirties. These hopes, of course, were dashed by the stock market crash and the Great Depression. Students are asked to decide whether the policies of the conservatives were responsible for either the prosperity or the Depression.

The conflicts over taxing and spending are discussed in Part II. Traditionalists wished to fight the Depression by permitting drastic automatic readjustments in wages and prices. But Keynesians believed only the federal government spending vast amounts of money could stop the Depression. Keynes himself predicted that spending on the order required to restore prosperity would never be politically feasible during peace time and he was right. Neither Hoover or Roosevelt represented either the orthodox economists or the Keynesian school; but their vastly different approaches to pragmatic issues are contrasted, the results of their policies are compared, and the multiplier is tested against the economic statistics of the era.

Part III examines several crucial battles waged over the welfare state. Students are taken to the Tennessee Valley and asked whether similar river projects should be initiated by the government. Wallace's famous pig-kill controversy introduces the issue of establishing acreage controls to help farmers at the consumers' expense. The forerunner of the war on poverty is analyzed in a chapter on the Farm Security Administration and the issue of who should pay for these programs is dealt with in a chapter on taxation. Finally, students examine the relationship between the fundamental law of the land, the popular will, and the power of the president by studying Roosevelt's 'judicial reform' bill and the controversies it aroused.

The last section of the book updates the issues of the past through an analysis of the current farm problem, the war on poverty, and the controversy in the sixties over cutting taxes. This book cannot be completely up to date because the manifestations of the crucial economic issues are constantly changing; but by the same token it can never be out of date, for the concepts and controversies essential to understanding the prosperity and depression decades are always basic to the issues of the day.

Table of Contents

UNIT I.
WHAT CAUSED THE DEPRESSION ?

Family albums with pictures of grandparents looking young and unfamiliar in their outdated clothes can reveal a great deal about life at that time. Many a great uncle paused in front of his gleaming Lincoln convertible to be recorded for posterity before seeing his stockbroker and learning more about his rapidly increasing income. Many a now stately aunt was photographed living it up at a college party, with a raccoon coat and expensive silk hosiery. These pictures and many others taken during the 1920's reflect the prosperity and atmosphere of optimism that pervaded this decade.

But moving further along in time the album should reveal the same people under very different circumstances. The great uncle might be one of many men standing with expressionless faces looking for jobs or waiting for relief checks. The aunt, possibly wearing the same dress, would reveal in the thinness of her face and the fear in her eyes the great tragedy of the 1930's.

What brought about the prosperity? Conservatives claim it was the economic policies of Presidents Harding, Coolidge, and Hoover, who balanced the budget, partially repaid America's war debts, reduced taxes, and cut back on government spending. What caused the depression that followed? Liberals claim there was an uneven prosperity in the 1920's which increased the wealth of the rich, which never trickled down to the farmers and the other poor people, and which failed to put enough purchasing power in the hands of people who would spend it to buy the wheat, the cars, the refrigerators, and the radios produced in the 1920's. This unit asks the reader to decide what caused the prosperity and then what caused the Depression.

1

Warren Gamaliel Harding (1865–1923)
Twenty-ninth President of the United States.

Chapter 1
Conservatism and Normalcy

Introduction

After two decades of reform (the Progressive Era), a crusade to Save the World for Democracy (World War I), and a purge of alleged leftist and enemy elements within the U.S. (the Red Scare), the American people turned away from progressivism and internationalism. In 1920 they elected Warren Harding, who was not identified with the reform movements of the previous decades. Harding gathered men around him who represented the economic ideas of businessmen and conservative thinkers. The policies they put into effect for the next twelve years are still associated with conservatives, and they are identified in this chapter so the reader may see their relationship to debates over the prosperity of the 1920's and the Depression that followed.

Warren Harding and Normalcy

The nomination and election of Warren Harding in 1920 signaled a return to economic ideas and social attitudes of the 1890's. Warren Harding was a small-town politician and newspaper editor, elected to the Senate, and propelled into the Republican nomination by a shrewd political boss, Harry Daugherty. Before the Republican convention of 1920, Daugherty had predicted Harding's nomination as a compromise or "dark horse" candidate. Daugherty's fantastic prophecy proved to be correct to the very hour in which the party bosses made their decision to nominate Harding. In the absence of a truly popular candidate, the bosses controlled the Republican convention, which dutifully ratified the choice made in a smoke-filled hotel room the night before.

What really made Harding presidential timber was the mood of a country that had tired of liberal reform. Harding had captured this mood in a famous speech in which he coined the word "normalcy," which caught the spirit of a decade: "America's present need is not heroism but healing;

3

not nostrums but normalcy; not revolution but restoration; not agitation but adjustment."[1]

It mattered little that the word "normalcy" was not in the English language, for the American voter longed to return to "the good old days" of the 1890's when President McKinley promised a "full dinner pail" and neither international responsibilities nor domestic reforms were the orders of the day. Harding's campaign speeches played on this longing. He plucked a favorite chord by taking a stand for "happiness" as the greatest thing in the world. In his rhapsodies on normalcy, he declared in favor of peace, honesty, private enterprise, Americanism, low taxes, and a balanced budget. He asked Europeans to repay their war debts to America and proposed raising tariffs to heights that made repayment impossible. He campaigned in the McKinley manner by remaining in his Ohio home where he received visiting delegations and played horseshoes. He was, in the words of one of his supporters, "no world beater," but he gave voice to a mood most Americans shared; and he was elected over the Democratic ticket of Cox and Roosevelt by an unprecedented 7-million vote margin.

Harding's three outstanding choices for the cabinet were: Herbert Hoover, millionaire, engineer, and humanitarian, Secretary of Commerce; Andrew Mellon, banker and industrialist, the third richest man in America and the wealthiest ever to become Secretary of the Treasury; Charles Evans Hughes, a former corporation lawyer and Supreme Court justice, Secretary of State. Some other cabinet posts and lesser offices, however, were handed to weak or dishonest men. Secretary of Interior Albert B. Fall and two friends were convicted of corruption that ran into hundreds of millions, and all three went to prison. Harding's campaign manager, Harry Daugherty, was appointed Attorney General and later accused of corruption. He was acquitted when a jury failed to reach a verdict after arguing for over sixty-six hours. Not since President Grant's day had the nation's capital been rocked by such enormous scandals. Harding died in 1923, just before these scandals broke, and Calvin Coolidge, his successor, provided a much needed honesty in the direction of the nation's affairs. However, the change from Harding to Coolidge did not alter the underlying philosophy of government, which was provided by Secretary of the Treasury Mellon.

Andrew Mellon Opposes High Taxes

No issue better illustrates the conservatism of the Republican leadership during the 1920's than the tax debate. The highest tax rate when Harding came to power was 73 percent. Normalcy to Harding and millions of his followers meant reducing taxes and paring down government expenses. Mellon, a Pittsburgh financier who had resigned sixty corporate directorships to take his cabinet post, proposed reducing the highest rate to 31 percent. The government, Mellon readily conceded, would suffer at least a temporary decrease in income from such a drastic reduction. Mellon himself would save millions. But in the long run, Mellon argued, high taxes are self-defeating because they destroy savings (capital) that are invested in business:

Our civilization, after all, is based on accumulated capital, and that capital is no less vital to our prosperity than is the extraordinary energy which has built up in this country the greatest material civilization the world has ever seen. Any policy that deliberately destroys that capital under the spur of necessity is striking directly at the soundness of our financial structure and is full of menace for the future.[2]

High taxes, Mellon argued, destroy incentive because men will not work if the government rakes off the profit. President Coolidge underscored this argument by asking how many days a man would work if the government took 5 percent of his salary the first day, 10 percent the second, and so on, until it demanded 60 percent on the sixth day. Free the businessman to earn money by allowing him to keep the money he earns and he will build factories that employ more workers, thereby developing the entire nation and benefiting everybody.

Mellon succeeded in winning Congress to his views in 1921; wartime excess-profits taxes were repealed and the highest tax bracket was reduced to 58 percent. But three years later, Democrats and liberal Republicans beat back Mellon's attempt to cut the surtax* to 25 percent. When taxes fall too hard on big incomes, Mellon had said, "ways will always be found to avoid taxes so destructive"; in fact, the higher surtaxes "have already passed the point where they can be collected."[3] Congressman La Follette denounced such tenderness for millionaires. "Brazenly and impudently," cried La Follette, Secretary Mellon claimed "wealth will not and cannot be made to bear its full share of taxation."[4] Congress approved La Follette's substitute tax bill, which cut the normal rate for smaller taxpayers in half while conceding only a small reduction in surtaxes on big incomes. The inheritance tax was pushed up from 25 percent to 40 percent, the highest yet.

Mellon and Coolidge denounced the new tax law, though the President signed it. Inheritance taxes, "carried to an excess," warned Mellon, "in no way differ from the methods . . . in Russia." He upheld the trickle-down theory: if a businessman "uses his abilities within the bounds of the moral sense of the community, [his] monetary success is not a crime"; he adds to "the total wealth" and to "an increase in the standard of living."[5]

Mellon's Triumph

In the 1924 elections, Coolidge and La Follette made the Mellon plan a major issue. La Follette led the ticket of a third party, the Progressives, that not only attacked the policies of normalcy but succeeded in winning nearly 5 million votes, breaking all records for a third party. Pro-Coolidge newspapers called La Follette a "Bolshevik," and Coolidge himself said the issue was "whether America will allow itself to be degraded into a communistic or socialistic state or whether it will remain American."[6]

Opponents of the Mellon plan claimed that business did not lack money to invest in industry, and they insisted that workers and farmers needed to be given higher incomes. Actually, reformers like the Progressive

---

*The surtaxes were the higher rates of taxation which increased as income increased. They were generally added to a normally flat percentage rate which everybody paid.

senators, La Follette and George Norris, and the Socialist Norman Thomas were advocating an enlarged economic role for the government: a government that would help consumers by moving against high prices held rigid by tacit agreement between business firms; a government that would help workers to better the unsatisfactory levels of real wages; a government that would intervene in areas afflicted with "sick industries" and depressed agriculture.

Coolidge and Mellon were sure that they scented a whiff of socialism in the complaints against normalcy. Though some estimates placed unemployment around 10 percent of the workers, Coolidge was horrified by the proposal for unemployment insurance, which he felt would give a worker money he did not earn. Mellon's main speech in the 1924 campaign praised the way Mussolini suppressed strikes by working men. Mellon was not for dictatorships, but he said Mussolini was sensibly trying to "reestablish the Italian government upon sound principles,"[7] by which he meant private enterprise.

Winning 54 percent of the popular vote in 1924, Coolidge could and did claim a mandate for the Mellon plan. The new Congress dutifully cut the highest surtax to 20 percent and the inheritance tax was cut in half. Mellon hoped soon to get the latter wholly eliminated, but otherwise his victory was complete. Senator George Norris of Nebraska called the Mellon bill indefensible. "It is a millionaire's bill"; nearly all reductions were on incomes of the "immensely wealthy." "Mr. Mellon himself gets a larger personal reduction than the aggregate [combined amount] of practically all the taxpayers in the state of Nebraska."[8] He argued that the cut in inheritance taxes was the greatest step backward since the war. Mellon was not disturbed by such attacks; he felt sure in his position that the diversion of investment money out of the Treasury and into productive

SELECTED TAX REDUCTIONS, 1918–1926

Act of 1918	*Act of 1921*	*Act of 1924*	*Act of 1926*
Income tax: normal rate			
4% on first $4000	Unchanged	2% on first $4000	1-1/2% on first $4000
8% on remainder		4% on second $4000	3% on second $4000
		6% on remainder	5% on remainder
Income tax: surtax			
52% on $100,000	48% on $100,000	37% on $100,000	20% above
to $150,000	to $150,000	to $200,000	$100,000
65% above	50% above	40% above	
$1,000,000	$200,000	$500,000	(see above)
Inheritance or estate tax			
25% above	Unchanged	40% above	20% above
$10,000,000		$10,000,000	$10,000,000

Adapted from: James C. Malin, *The United States after the World War* (Boston: Ginn and Co., 1930), pp. 104–105.

enterprise was the way to stimulate a business boom. Hence, to Mellon it was irrelevant that the tax burden for the Mellon family (including his brothers) on a taxable income of about $5 million a year was reduced under the 1926 law (as compared with the 1921 law) by about $2 million.

Mellon's triumph was more complete than his critics realized, for Treasury refunds due to big taxpayers were not publicized. Under Mellon's leadership, the Treasury, without publicity, returned to corporations and big taxpayers refunds totaling $3.5 billion. Several million dollars were refunded to Alcoa Aluminum, Gulf Oil, and other Mellon companies.

The Tariff

There was one variety of high tax rates that Mellon did not try to push down; tariff rates, in fact, went up to an all-time high.

Harding's congress, and Hoover's later on, thought tariffs would protect business firms, workers, and farmers from competition with cheap European labor; the low rates of 1913 shot up to a new high in the Fordney-McCumber Act of 1921, and higher still in the Hawley-Smoot Tariff of 1930. Dissenters like Senator Norris opposed the tariff raises on the grounds that they helped American industry to maintain unnecessarily high prices and that they hurt those manufacturers and farmers who needed to sell abroad.

Balancing the Budget

Mellon thought it was more important to release investment capital by cutting taxes than to keep taxes up in order to make larger payments to retire the national debt. But it was the magic of Mellon, his admirers contended, that he could balance the budget and pay some of the debt even while cutting taxes. Andrew Mellon, chorused countless businessmen, was "the greatest Secretary of the Treasury since Alexander Hamilton." Some thought him better than Hamilton. Despite tax cuts, the Treasury regularly had a surplus, out of which Mellon made moderate payments on the national debt, reducing it by $3 billion in his first eight years of office.

It would not have been possible to reduce taxes and balance the budget without economizing in government, and Mellon linked the three ideas. Spending for the army and navy was maintained at around 20 percent of government expenditure, public works were held down to 4 to 6 percent, interest on the national debt hovered around 27 percent, while 11 percent or so went to payments on the debt. Coolidge's budget message of 1928 estimated that only one-fifth of tax moneys went for civil functions; four-fifths went out for defense and past wars: veterans' care and pensions, debt left by war, and the army and navy. Budget pruning chiefly fell on education, research, and various social services. The cry to balance the budget while reducing taxes strengthened the resistance of Mellon and Coolidge to attempts to get aid for farmers, pensions for war veterans, and federal development of the Tennessee Valley.

The Philosophy of Laissez-Faire

More than mere budget pruning was involved in decisions to reduce social services. Mellon and his three presidents had a deep faith that the economy functions best when government does not interfere with the free market. This belief is called laissez-faire. Laissez-faire underscored the decision to keep the federal government out of the Tennessee Valley, out of the taxpayer's pocket, and out of the farmer's market. Interference by government, it was argued, would disrupt the natural laws that govern the economy, such as supply and demand, and cause men to depend on government rather than on themselves for economic welfare. By the same principle, laissez-faire in a business depression meant a layoff of workers, curtailment of production, and elimination of the weaker competitors who were forced into bankruptcy. The laissez-faire philosophy linked efficiency with the popular Darwinian theory of "survival of the fittest."

NOTES

1. Samuel Adams, *Incredible Era* (Boston: Houghton Mifflin Company, 1939), p. 17.
2. Andrew Mellon, *Taxation: The People's Business* (New York: The Macmillan Company, 1924), pp. 71–72.
3. Harvey O'Connor, *Mellon's Millions* (New York: Blue Ribbon Books, Inc., 1933), pp. 127, 133.
4. *Ibid.,* p. 127.
5. *Ibid.,* p. 136.
6. Malcom Moos, *The Republicans* (New York: Random House, 1956), p. 355.
7. Harvey O'Connor, *Op. Cit.,* p. 338.
8. George W. Norris, *Fighting Liberal* (New York: The Macmillan Company, 1945), p. 288.

QUESTIONS

1. How did Mellon's policies illustrate a businessman's ideas of 'normalcy'?

2. How were each of the following groups affected by budget-balancing policies and by changes in tariffs, estate taxes, and income taxes: men of large income; farmers; veterans; businessmen and farmers living in the Tennessee Valley? Which groups, in your judgment, needed more help than they were given? Which were given too much?

3. What effect do you think the policies of normalcy would have on the growth and general health of the economy?

SUGGESTED READING

General works on the 1920's include William Leuchtenburg, *Perils of Prosperity* (Chicago: University of Chicago Press, 1958), John D. Hicks, *Republican Ascendency, 1921–1933* (New York: Harper & Row, Publishers, Inc., 1960, 1963), Arthur M. Schlesinger, Jr. *The Crisis of the Old Order, 1919–1933* (Boston: Houghton Mifflin Company, 1957), Frederick Lewis Allen's sparkling *Only Yesterday* (New York: Harper & Row, Publishers, Inc., 1931), Samuel Hopkins Adam's sensational *Incredible Era: The Life and Times of Warren Gamaliel Harding* (Boston: Houghton

Mifflin Company, 1939), and Mark Sullivan's graphic *Our Times, The United States, 1900–1925,* Vol. VI (New York: Charles Scribner's Sons, 1935). Frederick L. Paxson, *American Democracy and the World War, Postwar Years, Normalcy, 1918–1923* (Berkeley: University of California Press, 1948) covers Harding's administration. Harvey O'Connor, *Mellon's Millions* (New York: Blue Ribbon Books, Inc., 1933) is caustic on tax policies. For oil scandals see Burl, Noggle, *Teapot Dome* (Baton Rouge: Louisiana State University Press, 1962).

Chapter 2
The Farm Problem

Introduction

Part and parcel of the policies pursued during the 1920's was the desire to limit the sphere of government activity. This desire was in direct conflict with the aims of those representing farmers who believed that agriculture presented a special case and that it required federal assistance. This chapter discusses the farmer's condition: what made the once independent yeoman request federal help? The reader will be asked to decide whether the government should aid farmers.

Farm Prosperity in Peace and War

"One American harvest would buy the kingdom of Belgium, king and all; two would buy Italy; three would buy Austria-Hungary; and five at spot cash prices would take Russia from the Czar," boasted a writer in a 1908 edition of *Wallace's Farmer*.[1] Indeed, times were good during the years preceding World War I. Farm prices had doubled in fifteen years, and farmers were paying their debts, improving their farms, and buying new land with their profits. Consumers found food prices uncomfortably high. Two presidents, Theodore Roosevelt and Howard Taft, feared that population was growing faster than production and that food would be in short supply. Farm population was decreasing rapidly in proportion to total population, and food exports were decreasing. James J. Hill, president of the Great Northern Railroad, actually forecast a "nation-wide famine" within twenty-five years.[2] High farm prices undoubtedly reflected this increased demand and shortened supply.

On June 28, 1914, a tubercular and emotionally disturbed Serbian student assassinated Archduke Francis Ferdinand, heir to the throne of Austria-Hungary. Within five weeks, Europe was at war. As armies trampled over European fields and farmers were called away from their plows, the demand for American agricultural products increased spectacularly. Germany soon closed the Dardanelles, depriving Britain of her supply of

10

Farm Income, 1910–1947

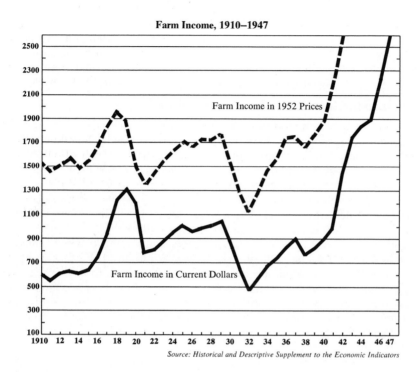

Source: Historical and Descriptive Supplement to the Economic Indicators

Russian wheat; at the same time an acute shipping shortage halted her grain and beef shipments from Argentina. American farmers were asked to fill the Allies' demand.

Prices of farm commodities rose spectacularly. Wheat prices climbed from the pre-war figure of $1.00 a bushel to $1.60, reached a high of $3.43 in December, 1916, and stabilized at $2.20 in 1918. Hogs, which had brought $8.00 a hundredweight when the war broke out, reached $18.00. The total value of American farm products rose from an average of $6 billion in the years immediately preceding the war to $13 billion in 1917 and $17 billion in 1919.

These high prices stimulated farm production. Land once considered too unproductive to farm became profitable with $2.00 wheat and farmers not only planted previously abandoned acres, but put the plow to new lands. According to one estimate, 45 million acres were opened up under the stimulation of war-time prices. By 1915, farmers harvested a billion bushels of wheat, a harvest unequaled during the next decade. Though an epidemic of black rust and temporary low prices decreased wheat production over the following years, acreage increased, and by 1919 farmers were harvesting 75 million acres.

At the war's end, American farmers found themselves greatly over-extended. The question then was how long war-time demand and prices would hold up. During 1919, Europeans continued to rely on American farm products to feed their hungry people. But soon normal trade routes were restored, soldiers on the continent returned to their farms, and European agriculture was back on its feet.

Overproduction Causes Low Farm Prices

Prices of farm commodities fell sharply. Wheat, which had sold for $2.15 a bushel in December of 1919, fell to $1.44 by the next Christmas and to $.92 by 1921. Similarly, corn prices dropped from a high of $1.35 to a low of $.42 a bushel, and cotton fell to one-third of its 1919 high. Total farm income tumbled disastrously from $17 billion to $7 billion.

Rapidly declining farm prices might have been less demoralizing if prices of other commodities had also declined, but farmers were alone in their agony, for while deflation struck agriculture, inflation lifted non-farm retail prices to record levels. Farmers' purchasing power eventually reached a scant 63 percent of 1913 levels. While in 1919 a farmer could earn enough money from the sale of one bushel of corn to buy five gallons of gasoline, two years later it took ten bushels to buy the same amount of gas. While six bushels of corn bought a ton of coal in 1919, it took sixty bushels to buy a ton of coal in 1921. Small wonder that farmers found it cheaper to burn corn rather than buy coal. (Unfortunately, corn did not fit into the gas tank.)

Farm costs, too, remained high. Property values had increased 70 percent during flush times, almost paralleling rising prices. When prices failed to fall following the armistice in November, 1918, farmers were convinced a new price plateau had been reached despite occasional warnings to the contrary. Consequently, savings were invested in land, whose values occasionally reached speculative heights. A similar boom occurred in livestock where, for example, a single breeding bull, named Rag Apple

WHEAT PRODUCTION AND PRICES

	Price per bushel (dollars)	Production (1000 bu.)	Acreage (1000 acres)
1910	.91	625,476	45,793
1916	1.43	634,572	53,510
1918	2.05	904,130	61,068
1919	2.16	952,097	73,700
1920	1.83	843,277	62,358
1922	.97	846,649	61,397
1924	1.25	841,617	52,463
1926	1.21	832,213	56,616
1928	1.00	914,373	59,226
1930	.67	886,522	62,637

Source: United States Bureau of the Census, *Historical Statistics of the United States, 1789–1945* (Washington, D.C., 1949), p. 106.

the Great, brought $125,000. To pay for land, livestock, and improvements, farmers borrowed heavily; their total indebtedness increased by $5.5 billion during the war years, reaching $10.2 billion by 1920. Taxes and mortgages, based on war values, more than doubled the farmers' prewar debts. Freight rates and farm wages paid to hired hands also increased, adding to the farmer's woes. Although new machines increased productivity, payments were made on them from shrinking revenues. After the war ended, returning servicemen bought farms at inflated rates. They suffered along with everyone else when the crash came.

The Farm Problem

In 1929, enough wealth was produced in the United States to grant every man, woman, and child an income of $716, but the per capita income of farmers lagged at $168. There were other inequities. Compared to the city dweller, the farmer paid more than his proportionate share of taxes and had worse roads, schools, and public services. Hospitals, doctors, and public-health facilities usually did not exist in the country. As over two-thirds of all farmers lived more than five miles away from towns (and usually towns with a population of 2500 or less) amusements also were rare. In 1930, only 9.2 percent of farms had electricity, 4.5 percent had radios, and 10 percent enjoyed indoor plumbing. During the 1920's, 2 million disgruntled farmers left their homes each year. Though this exodus was counterbalanced by an influx and by high birth rates, total farm population actually decreased by 1.5 million during this time.

Laissez-faire spokesmen thought farmers could blame no one but themselves for their problems. "If they would only plant as much as they know they can sell," mused Bernard Baruch, a Wall Street colossus who became concerned over the farmer's plight. No one had forced farmers to increase their acreage by borrowing money in order to buy machinery and new lands. The farmer had made his money when times were good and should have had the foresight to avoid overproduction. The free enterprise system would solve the problem. Big farmers, concluded Baruch, were effi-

PRICES AND FARM INCOME

	Hog price per 100 lbs. (dollars)	Cotton price per 100 lbs. (dollars)	Prices rec'd by farmers	Prices paid by farmers	Parity ratio
1910	8.14	13.96	102	96	106
1916	8.37	17.36	118	125	94
1918	16.14	28.88	204	173	118
1920	12.92	15.89	211	202	104
1924	7.34	22.91	143	167	86
1928	8.54	17.98	151	168	90
1930	8.84	9.46	128	160	80

Source: United States Bureau of the Census, *Historical Statistics of the United States, 1789–1945* (Washington, D.C., 1949), pp. 99, 101, 108.

cient. In the case of small farmers who were not efficient, they needed "help"; but "our objective should be steadily to reduce them and ultimately eliminate them." Reduction of the number of farmers would reduce production, farm prices would rise, and efficient farmers would prosper.

The farmers held another view. They felt that they were victims of circumstances beyond their control. When foreign markets opened during the war, they were urged to expand production to meet the Allies' need for food. Now that the new markets were closed to America, farmers were unable to cut back production in the way businessmen reduced theirs; for how could millions of farmers get together and agree to reduce their crops? If one farmer limited his planting, he would sell less and earn less without creating the scarcity that raises prices. Arguments about leaving the farm seemed rather heartless. Where would the farmer go? Who would buy his farm? And how could he adjust to life in the city?

Peek and Johnson Propose Help for the Farmer

Some people, worried by the economic squeeze on the farmer, said that farm prosperity was important to businessmen as well as farmers. George Peek and Hugh Johnson had taken control of the Moline Plow Company right after World War I and, following several unsuccessful years, decided they could not make a profit until farmers again were prosperous, for "you can't sell a plow to a busted farmer." In 1922 they collaborated on a pamphlet, "Equality for Agriculture," which proposed a plan to raise farmers' purchasing power to the prosperous 1910–1914 levels. They wanted a government Farm Board to take the surpluses off the farmers' hands and sell them overseas at the going price. The remaining farm products would be sold by farmers in the United States at a higher price protected by the tariff. In this way, farmers would benefit from the high tariffs that also protected industry from foreign competition.

Let us use wheat to illustrate how the Peek-Johnson plan was to work. Farmers harvested approximately 800 million bushels of wheat, 100 million more than they could sell in the United States. The surplus was sold overseas at $1.00 a bushel and the domestic price usually fell to the same level. If some way could be found to sell the surplus abroad and prevent importation of foreign wheat, the remaining wheat could be sold at home for a higher price. A 42-cent tariff protecting American wheat from foreign competition would enable producers to raise the home price to $1.42 before foreigners could import wheat.

Peek's plan provided that the Farm Bureau would buy the surplus 100 million bushels and sell it abroad for $1.00 a bushel (or $100 million). The remaining 700 million bushels would then sell at home for $994 million ($1.42 × 700,000,000), making the total income from wheat $1094 million. This income represented a $294 million increase over the old harvest of $800 million. To repay the Farm Bureau for the losses it would suffer by buying wheat at $1.42 and selling it for $1.00, farmers would be charged a 6-cent equalization fee. Why 6 cents? Because this would divide the $42 million government loss equally among the 700 million bushels protected in the home market.

This proposal would give American farmers advantages over competitors in Argentina and Canada. American farmers would get more money for their wheat, overseas peoples would get American wheat at the depressed world price, and the government would be paid for its losses through the equalization fee. Who would then foot the bill? The American consumer who bought the bread and paid good money for it. But his costs would be relatively slight. A pound loaf of bread contained less than 2 cents worth of wheat at prevailing prices and less than 3 cents when wheat reached $1.42.

McNary and Haugen Sponsor Equalization Bill

Harding's appointee as Secretary of Agriculture, Henry C. Wallace, was so impressed with Peek's equalization scheme that he had it drawn up into a bill which Representative Gilbert Haugen (Iowa) and Senator Charles McNary (Oregon) introduced to Congress on January 16, 1924. In its original form, the McNary-Haugen Bill was to cover wheat, flour, rice, corn, wool, cattle, sheep, and swine. It was endorsed by over 200 farm agencies, but the House of Representatives rejected the bill 233 to 153. This, however, was not the end of the bill. It was re-introduced, in slightly different forms, every year between 1925 and 1928. In 1925, it was reported favorably by the agricultural committee, but was caught in the rush for adjournment and failed to come to a vote. It was again defeated in 1926. The McNary-Haugen measure passed both houses of Congress in 1927 but was vetoed by President Calvin Coolidge.

The opposition to the McNary-Haugen bill fell into several camps. Many, agreeing in principle, simply believed the idea unworkable. More substantial opposition came from men who feared any extension of the economic role of the government and from people particularly opposed to increasing farm income through artificial price supports.

It was impolitic for critics of the McNary-Haugen bill to say openly that the farmer had best be left to his own devices, because 25 percent of all voters still lived on farms. Yet, behind much criticism of equalization proposals was the assumption that government should not interfere with the law of supply and demand, and that the solution for the overproduction causing the farm depression was greater crop diversification and, even more important, fewer farmers. Opponents of agricultural reform advocated cooperative marketing, a solution involving a minimum of government interference and no change in consumer prices.

Secretary of Treasury Andrew Mellon came to bat for the administration in 1926, sending Congress a letter criticizing the McNary-Haugen bill. He warned that increasing farm prices would stimulate agricultural production without increasing consumption. Mellon also objected that subsidizing farmers would establish a dangerous precedent, for you could not refuse help to "the textile, boot and shoe, coal, and other industries which are finding some difficulty in disposing of their surplus." Finally, once you have aided the farmer, "the natural result of the bill will be to increase production" and "the unfortunate condition of the farmer will be aggravated and not improved" for government cannot "successfully oppose fundamental economic laws.[3]

The issue was whether there was a national responsibility under which a government should find ways to deal with serious economic fluctuations; farming was a sick industry. Farmers demanded assistance and the McNary-Haugen bill attempted to answer this demand by providing that the government buy farm surpluses and sell them abroad. Government intervention was opposed by men like Andrew Mellon, who felt that the farm problem would be solved only when enough farmers abandoned their way of life and took work in the city. Was Mellon right in leaving farmers to solve their own probelms? Or should the federal government have taken action to help them? The same issue was again to appear in the years of depression and is treated in later chapters.

NOTES

1. Theodore Saloutos and John Hicks, *Agricultural Discontent in the Middle West* (Madison: University of Wisconsin Press, 1951), p. 20.

2. *Ibid.,* p. 27.

3. Andrew Mellon in a letter to Haugen in William Sutherland (ed.), *Debate Handbook in the McNary-Haugen Agricultural Surplus Control Act* (Lexington: University of Kentucky Press, 1927), pp. 318, 320.

QUESTIONS

1. Andrew Mellon would argue that the unfortunate effect of high farm prices is increased farm production. Do you think this statement is true?

2. Is it realistic to say that the best solution for the farm problem is for the unsuccessful to quit farming? Explain your answer.

3. Does the federal government have an obligation to help farmers? Why or why not?

SUGGESTED READING

Murray R. Benedict, *Farm Policies of the United States, 1790–1950* (New York: Twentieth Century Fund, 1953) presents a wealth of information. James H. Shideler analyzes the disruption of agriculture caused by World War I in *Farm Crisis, 1919–1923* (Berkeley: University of California Press, 1957). Gilbert C. Fite covers the McNary-Haugen controversy in *George N. Peek and the Fight for Farm Parity* (Norman, Oklahoma: University of Oklahoma Press, 1952). Theodore Saloutos and John D. Hicks, *Agricultural Discontent in the Middle West* (Madison: University of Wisconsin Press, 1951) is a standard reference.

Chapter 3
Prosperity : Fact or Myth

Introduction

The irresistible attraction of Andrew Mellon's conservative economic policies was that they seemed to work; good times abounded in the 1920's. True, farmers and miners did not share in the general prosperity, and business profits increased much faster than wages, but more Americans had more stocks, more debts, and more shiny new gadgets in 1929 than ever before. A middle-class city dweller probably owned a car, a radio, lived in his own house, had savings in the bank, and set money aside to send his children to college. And he probably shared the growing conviction that the United States was about to do the impossible: abolish poverty.

City dwellers were not very distressed that farmers weren't prospering—couldn't the farmer migrate to the city? that many people were poor—wouldn't prosperity eventually "trickle down" to them? that stock prices were peaking at dizzy heights—wasn't the market a reflection of confidence in the future?

Time has given the viewer a longer perspective. And social scientists have provided data not known to the government or the public in the 1920's. In hindsight, was the prosperity of the 1920's only a golden illusion? Were there weak spots in the economy which foreshadowed the Depression that followed? This chapter will help answer these questions.

The New Ford

The date was December 2, 1927. The grand event was the first showing of the brand new Model A Ford, which Americans and Europeans had been excitedly awaiting for eighteen months. In New York 1 million people waited eagerly outside the seventy-six Ford showrooms. In Detroit, 100 thousand people stormed a dealer's showroom. In Madrid, nearly 150 thousand Spaniards attended the showing. In Berlin, the police had to fight back the crowds outside the exhibition rooms.

17

There was good reason for the excitement. Henry Ford had long produced the most popular and the cheapest car in the United States. For eighteen years his Model T dominated the automobile market; its sales totaled more than 15 million vehicles. The Model T outlasted other cars by an average of nearly two years and undersold its nearest competitor by over $100. Between 1921 and 1926, it held 40 percent of the market. When Ford abruptly dismissed 100 thousand workers to retool for his new model, Americans waited patiently. Many put off buying another car until they could inspect the new model Ford. Four hundred thousand people had such faith in Henry Ford that they ordered the Model A before it was off the drawing board and on the assembly line.

The Model A was a definite improvement over the Model T. The new Ford had a three-speed transmission in place of the old planetary type, which required one foot on the pedal to keep in low gear. The new Ford was lower, faster, and more comfortable. It could develop a top speed of 65 miles an hour with a 45-horsepower engine, compared to the 40 mile-an-hour speed and 40 horsepower of the older car. The Model A was the only low-priced car with hydraulic shock absorbers, which gave it a smooth ride instead of the bone-shaking discomfort of the Model T. While, as Ford once said, you could have the old tin lizzie in any color so long as it was black, the new Ford was available in Niagara and gun blue, Dawn gray and Arabian sand. The price of the new car was almost the same as the old. New Yorkers were so favorably impressed that on the first day they ordered 50 thousand.

More and Better Cars

In 1919, 6,771,074 passenger vehicles were registered in the United States. Ten years later this figure had leapt to 23,122,100, almost one car per family. Indeed, as surveys showed, many families bought cars before they installed bathtubs.

The cars of 1929 were cheaper than those of 1919, averaging $621 as compared to $888; they were also better, faster, and flashier. Production in 1929 reached over 4.58 million vehicles, tripling the 1919 mark. Americans produced seven-eighths of the world's cars, exporting one-half million vehicles each year. With an average of 4.6 persons per car, the United States far outdistanced all other nations in automobile ownership.

Impact of the Automobile

The shoe industry felt the impact of the automobile as people rode rather than walked, and wore out tires instead of shoes. But the automobiles did require replacement parts and services as well. Filling stations came to decorate the landscape, accompanied by billboards, roadside hot dog stands, restaurants, and camp sites. The automobile motorized crime; bootleggers ran whiskey hidden under the seats of old Fords, bank robbers could attempt their getaways in stolen Pierce Arrows, pursued by policemen in hopped-up Chevys. The railroads found they couldn't compete with cars, busses, and trucks; they either folded or began their long decline. Americans discovered they could live farther from the center of cities and hastened their long motor cavalcade toward suburbia. Farmers marketed eggs in the backs of their old Model T's and trucked vegetables and dairy products to the cities. Even courtship patterns were greatly influenced by the automobile; the car replaced the parlor as the place where pleading suitors "popped the question," and no survey was needed to discover why a man's popularity increased if he drove a new car.

By 1926, Americans were spending $6 billion yearly on purchases connected with their new motorized toys. Production of automobiles alone accounted for 12.7 percent of all manufacturing done in the country. Motor vehicles consumed 85 percent of our rubber imports, 67 percent of our plate glass, 19 percent of our iron and steel, and healthy percentages of our copper, hardwood lumber, and lead. Ten percent of the country's labor force was employed in making cars.

Billions were lavished on developments stimulated by the automobile. State and federal governments spent $1 billion annually building roads; local and city governments contributed half that sum. Thousands of additional developments were fostered by the automobile. Restaurants, resorts, tourist camps, and vacation spots were built to serve the customers brought by the automobile from all over the country. Small wonder that economists have pronounced the automobile "the main prop under the economy."[1]

Production, Profits, and Wages

America's claim to prosperity during the 1920's, or the automobile industry's leadership, with a profit rate of 19.7 percent was undisputed. Between 1920 and 1929, national income shot up by $22 billion, from $60 billion to $82 billion. Productivity, the amount produced in each working hour, increased by 25 percent during the 1920's at a rate of 3.5 percent a year. This spectacular gain in the worker's efficiency permitted a 15 percent per capita gain in real wages, mostly recorded between 1920 and 1923. It also allowed for increased business profits, a 62 percent rise in corporate earnings, and a doubling of dividend payments.

During the 1920's the average American's income went up by 20 percent. This gave him the money to purchase 27 million automobiles, and 3.5 million new homes. Nine million homes were wired for electricity, 6 million phones were installed, and 7 million radios were sold. School and college enrollments increased 75 percent. Of course, not all of this was paid for; mortgages aside, installment purchases increased by $6 billion. However, total indebtedness did not increase; savings actually doubled during the 1920's.

In 1920, the first radio sets appeared on the market. By 1922, sales totaled $60 million, but the craze had not yet really caught on. Over the next two years, sales more than doubled, and by 1929, Americans had spent $3.4 billion on radios. The radio story was repeated, though less dramatically, by countless other industries. Everywhere one looked new and improved products and gadgets began competing for the dollar. Moviemakers glamorized their products by introducing the public to stars such

WAGE RATES, UNION AND NON-UNION; AND UNEMPLOYMENT TOTALS

Average Hourly Earnings, 1920–1929

	Building trades (union workers)	Manufacturing (production workers)	Unskilled labor	Southern common labor	Cotton textiles (women spinners)	Labor force unemployed (in thousands)
1920—	$1.05		$.48	$.40	$.43	558
1921—	1.08		.37			4754
1922—	1.00		.36	.25	.30	2917
1923—	1.11	$.52	.41			749
1924—	1.19	.55	.41	.28	.32	2034
1925—	1.23	.55	.43			817
1926—	1.31	.55	.43	.28	.28	464
1927—		.55				1620
1928—		.56			.28	1857
1929—		.57		.28		429*

Source: United States Bureau of the Census, *Historical Statistics of the United States, 1789–1945* (Washington, D.C., 1949), pp. 68–71. Complete figures not available.

*The Bureau of Labor Statistics lists unemployment in 1929 at 1,499,000.

as Douglas Fairbanks and Mary Pickford, wooing all America into new film palaces. Figures of weekly theater attendance exceeded the total population; every man, woman, and child in this country averaged more than one movie show a week. The new electric power industry shared in the prosperity, along with rayons, cosmetics, cigarettes, telephones, refrigerators, and airplanes. Here lay the foundations of American affluence.

The Stock Market Jumps

A stock market boom was built on the foundations of this wealth. Nourished by corporate profits and dividends, and encouraged by government policies, stock prices began rising. Between 1921 and 1925 prices of common stock doubled. But the market had not yet become America's great passion; it did not make news considered worthy of front-page coverage and was content with trading a million shares a day. In 1927, however, speculators started paying earnest attention to the market, and they saw great possibilities. As they started buying heavily, the market shot skyward, with some stocks vaulting ten or twenty points in a single day. By 1928, common stocks averaged three times their 1921 values and still were being bid up. The market, many insiders thought, had reached a permanently high plateau. Brokers, bankers, and even government officials assured the public that stocks were not too high and would keep going up. Over 1 million Americans became financially committed to the market. Many had invested their life's savings; an estimated 600 thousand had borrowed to pay for their shares of stock. Stock sales regularly exceeded 5 million shares a day and the market was often front-page news. Profits were not made on the dividends paid, but on the increases in the market value of the shares themselves.

No Sugar Pills *or* Panaceas

THE outstanding problem of agriculture is *surplus* disposal. Which is a *selling* problem. And *also* the problem of *all* commerce.

Nobody knows *that* better than Herbert Hoover, the sales-expert.

He was born among the grain fields.

He chored in the grain fields.

As national Food Administrator and international bread-box filler, he mobilized the grain fields and put them in khaki.

For six years he was the biggest grain dealer in *history*.

He bought and sold and shipped *more* wheat and corn than any country annually consumes.

He knows the productivity of *every* grange, its traffic and its elevator facilities. He knows regional working costs, profit and dockage averages.

He knows that Federal legislation owes agriculture economic equality, protected markets and government cooperation.

And as *President*, Herbert Hoover will *secure* them.

He has *endorsed* no *specific* plan for farm relief, but he has *specifically* declared for the best *possible* plan.

And no experience is *better* equipped to recognize it.

His executive approval and party influence are pledged to make farming more *efficient* and *profitable*.

But the Republican platform and the candidate both insist that relief measures must be constructive, fundamental *and within Constitutional limits*—an honest *remedy*, not a *sugar-pill*.

Vote hunger has not inspired him to issue worthless campaign checks on Congressional authority. He has not promised from the *stump* what he cannot deliver from *office*.

The White House owes agriculture not only executive *sympathy* with its difficulties, but the practical training and the organization capacity to *overcome* them.

And Herbert Hoover is the *one* man for the job.

His analytical genius, his engineering mind, his organizing talent, and his scientific thoroughness cannot be tempted to espouse a half-cocked, jerry-built program.

Agriculture's cry for consideration will never be stilled with subsidy *soothing syrups*.

Agriculture must be reorganized, must be *rebuilt* into an efficient unit, with stabilized outlets, ready and steady credit.

It must learn to keep accounts and budgets, to *diversify* and rotate crops, improve herds and income with better sires and silos—it must be shown the dividends hidden in *chaff-pile*, churn and chicken coop. It must be taught to stick tools in the *hands* of the *clock* and give every hour a productive task.

That sort of thing is Herbert Hoover's *specialty*.

He will put agriculture on a sound footing—tighten its loose screws, plug its leaks, substitute *calculation* for *guess-work*, introduce cost engineering, and straighten the *wasteful* kinks out of distribution.

He needs no intermediaries to interpret the significance of *rural* prosperity to *national* prosperity.

He speaks the *farmer's language*, just as he speaks the *dialects* of merchandising and diplomacy, mining and hydro-electrics, radio and aviation, manufacturing and railroading, finance and export, science and lumbering, construction and conservation—the speech of *action* and *enterprise*.

His calibre and his character have been *universally* tested by emergency and responsibility.

His record establishes him as the *foremost American* and our *most useful citizen*.

He realizes every ideal of *true* democracy.

The Republican Party prides itself in presenting
HERBERT HOOVER
for President of the United States

PAID FOR BY THE UPTOWN TEXTILE ASSOCIATION, 468 FOURTH AVENUE

Those wishing to see similar advertisements in other New York papers may send cheques to the Republican Business Men, Inc., 4 West 40th Street

GENERAL COMMITTEE
George Henry Payne, Chairman

L. F. Loree	Samuel M. Vauclain	Wm. H. Hamilton	Julius Rosenwald	Albert Z. Gray	Edson S. Lott	F. H. McKnight	Wm. Cooper Procter	R. B. Strasburger
George Whitney	Henry Rogers Winthrop	Frank C. Munson	J. Horace Harding	Gen. W. W. Atterbury	Wm. Ziegler, Jr.	Kermit Roosevelt	Edmond E. Wise	Albert Forsch
Jules S. Bache				Herbert N. Straus				John B. Trevor

PERCENTAGE OF NATIONAL PERSONAL INCOME RECEIVED BY EACH
INCOME-TENTH BEFORE TAXES, 1910–1937

	Highest	2nd	3rd	4th	5th	6th	7th	8th	9th	Lowest
1910	33.9	12.3	10.2	8.8	8.0	7.0	6.0	5.5	4.9	3.4
1918	34.5	12.9	9.6	8.7	7.7	7.2	6.9	5.7	4.4	2.4
1921	38.2	12.8	10.5	8.9	7.4	6.5	5.9	4.6	3.2	2.0
1929	39.0	12.3	9.8	9.0	7.9	6.5	5.5	4.6	3.6	1.8

Source: Gabriel Kolko, *Wealth and Power in America* (New York: Frederick A.
Praeger, 1962), p. 14.

So much money was being made on the market that many corporations
found it more profitable to buy stocks than expand production. By 1929,
common stocks sold for four times their 1921 prices, but no one worried,
for the country had been suffering a depression in 1921 and now was riding
high on a crest of prosperity. Stock values, it was thought, reflected the
condition of the American economy. And, in a way, perhaps they did.

Prosperity is Uneven

The casual observer could uncover other signs of abundance. The number of people paying taxes on incomes of $1 million or more was rapidly
increasing. In 1924, only seventy-five men were able to declare million-
dollar incomes; three years later, this number had risen to 283. But the
gains of the wealthy were not limited to a select class of millionaires. The
1 percent earning most money found their share of income was increasing
to about 14 percent during the 1920's; those in the upper 5 percent were
recording a greater gain, and by 1929 received over 25 percent of all the
nation's income. Indeed, Americans were suffering a distribution problem.
The richest 36,000 families had incomes equivalent to the earnings of the
poorest 12 million. But these figures did not shock very many, for it was

PERCENTAGE SHARES OF TOP, MIDDLE, AND LOWER INCOME GROUPS IN
TOTAL NONFARM INCOME, 1920–1929

	Top 1 percent	Next 6 percent	Lower 93 percent
1920	12.87	12.90	74.23
1921	13.49	15.12	71.39
1922	13.41	14.56	72.03
1923	12.37	13.59	74.04
1924	13.04	14.75	72.21
1925	13.99	15.20	70.81
1926	14.06	14.96	70.98
1927	14.66	15.25	70.09
1928	15.19	15.60	69.21
1929	14.76	15.29	69.95

Source: Simon Kuznets, *Shares of Upper Income Groups in Income and Savings,*
National Bureau of Economic Research, 1953, Table 116. Net realized capital gains
and losses are excluded.

thought the poor were also getting wealthier, though, admittedly, at a slower rate.

Yet, many Americans could not help but see the blemishes in this picture. Not everyone was prosperous. Certainly not the farmers, who were buried under a surplus of wheat, cotton, and corn; nor the miners, who found the need for coal slacking while unsold surpluses mounted. Textile and leather workers, too, were overproducing and could not command prosperity wages. Doctors and lawyers in 1929 had average net incomes a bit over $5000. The best-paid city school teachers received $2000 or more, but rural grade-school and some high-school teachers received as little income as workmen, who averaged only $1500. Estimates of a family minimum income necessary for "health and decency" ranged between $1820 and $2080.

Not everything glittered in the Golden Twenties. In 1929, 1,900 rubber workers in Hartford and New Haven lost their jobs because production was shifted to more efficient factories run elsewhere by the same companies. After eleven months, 13 percent of these men were still looking for work, and 66 percent had to accept lower-paying positions. They could take small comfort in the knowledge they were not alone. Increased industrial efficiency, call it technological unemployment or automation, had eliminated over 3.25 million jobs during the 1920's, or about 900 each day for ten years. Though most displaced workers were eventually able to find employment, this usually meant months of searching and eventually settling for lower wages. Since the working force grew faster than the number of new jobs, looking for work seemed more and more like a game of musical chairs—when the music stopped there just weren't enough places for everyone.

Fact or Myth

In 1928, Herbert Hoover, the Republican presidential candidate, predicted that the United States was nearing the time when she would conquer poverty. Hoover pointed proudly to the statistics showing that national income was rising and concluded that more Americans were enjoying more of the material rewards of life than ever before. The future looked rosy, and Hoover credited the conservative policies of the past eight years. The nation endorsed his judgment with a resounding vote of confidence in the November presidential election of 1928.

NOTE

1. Allan Nevins, *Ford: Expansion and Challenge, 1915–32* (New York: Charles Scribner's Sons, 1957), p. 381.

QUESTIONS

1. Do you think Mellon's tax policies may have stimulated a boom in the automobile industry and that the auto boom stimulated a boom in the economy? Why or why not?

2. Do you think America's economy was healthy during the 1920's? Explain.

3. Were there any danger signals that might spell trouble in the future? Explain.

4. What steps, if any, by taxes or other measures, do you think a government should take in dealing with the distribution of prosperity? Explain your answers.

SUGGESTED READING

George H. Soule presents an economic history of the 1920's emphasizing business performance in *Prosperity Decade: From War to Depression, 1917–1929* (New York: Rinehart and Company, Inc., 1947). In *Prosperity: Fact or Myth* (New York: A & C Boni, 1930) Stuart Chase poses the question few thought to ask during the 1920's. Chapters 7 and 11 of Frederick Lewis Allen's *Only Yesterday* (Harper & Row, Publishers, Inc., 1931) are very useful. A readable contemporary analysis is W. Z. Ripley, *Main Street and Wall Street* (Boston: Little, Brown and Company, 1927). For businessmen's views see J. W. Prothro, *Dollar Decade* (Baton Rouge: Louisiana State University Press, 1954).

Chapter 4
Rise and Crash

Introduction

In the mid-1920's a real-estate boom struck Florida. Land values soared. Fantastic sums were paid for swamplands; properties neatly divided into lots were sold from blueprints to buyers who never bothered to inspect their new acquisitions. This madness continued for two years until the hurricane of 1926 destroyed the speculative orgy.

A short time later, a similar boom beset the New York stock market and for eighteen months the market's climb paralleled the Florida boom. During this thrilling year and a half, as self-proclaimed prophets predicted even higher stock values, an encouraged public made their predictions come true by piling savings into the market and pushing stock prices sky-high. But the end came suddenly, raining more destruction on the market than the hurricane did on Florida's real-estate speculations.

This market boom was an important chapter in the history of the 1920's. It was fed by industry's high profits, by the savings of the rich, and by widespread speculation and borrowing. It created an illusion of prosperity real only to those with enough self-discipline to sell out in time to turn paper profits into hard cash. Finally, the repercussions of the crash signaled the end of the prosperity decade.

This chapter explains the workings of the stock market, as it defied all experts and climbed to unprecedented heights in 1929 and then plunged to unexpected depths a short time later. Since the market's rise and fall were so bound to the uneven prosperity of the 1920's and the depression that followed, it is impossible to comprehend this period without understanding the market.

What Are Stocks?

A stock is a certificate of a share of ownership in a business corporation, entitling its owner to dividends, that is, a share of the profits, and to a vote in that firm. Few people, however, ever attend the annual stockholder's

25

meeting where changes in policy are voted on and the top officers of the company are elected. Why, then, do they buy stocks? There are two good reasons: the first is the cash received in the form of dividends; the second is the hope that the stock's value will be bid up in the stock market so that the stock can be sold at a higher price than the owner paid for it.

Speculators and Investors

Between 1908 and 1928, common stocks were an excellent form of investment, and brokers and public figures were happy to make this known. As John J. Raskob, Democratic vice-presidential candidate in 1928 and a General Motors executive, explained in a magazine article, "Everyone Ought To Be Rich," the way to easy riches was buying stocks. He gave several convincing examples. Stock in General Motors purchased for $10,000 in 1918 was worth $16 million on the market 10 years later. Anyone who invested $15 each month for 20 years (or $3,600) in good common stock would have had a fortune of $80,000 by 1928. From these facts, Mr. Raskob concluded that everyone could and ought to be wealthy, for everyone could invest a small portion of his income in stocks every month.

Brokers who knew the stock market at least as well as John Raskob were often more conservative in their advice to clients. Don't buy stock, they cautioned, unless the stock's earnings are at least 10 percent of its purchase price. In other words, you should not pay more than $75 for a stock earning $7.50. This 10:1 ratio did not interest speculators, who preferred gambling on a future rise of stock values to investing in stock dividends. The speculator played the market like a man betting the horses. He would hope to buy low and sell high, for the speculator's way to riches was not to collect dividends based on a firm's earnings, but to bet on his stock's performance in the market.

The Market Begins to Rise

In 1928 the stock market made a sudden and spectacular rise. And yet, in the winter of 1927–28 most brokers were cautioning their clients not to buy stock, for according to the 10:1 rule, stock prices were already too high and needed readjustment downward before conditions warranted a plunge into the market.

However, a shrewd broker, Michael J. Meehan, was quite willing to gamble on the market. Meehan's firm owned a seat on the stock exchange and he worked on the floor of the exchange. His job involved two important duties. First, he filled out customer's orders relayed to him through his firm's offices; second, he specialized in Radio (RCA) stock. When other exchange members wanted to fill their customers' orders for Radio stock, they would buy it or sell it through Meehan. If asked for 100 shares of Radio, Meehan would find a seller and arrange for the sale. If no seller was immediately available, he would sell shares he owned personally. Upon completion, each sale was recorded on the stock-market ticker tape; for example, the sale of 200 shares of RCA at $94.50 each would be noted on the tape as RCA 2.94½. Every day the newspapers reported the open-

On *the* Peaks *of* Prosperity

THE Constitution of the United States was framed without special entrances to power and preference.

It cancelled *silver spoon birth-rights* and dropped a pass key to *all* public and private office into every cradle.

The underwriters of our independence abolished *preferred* shares and issued common stock to *everybody.*

They designed a cooperative enterprise, granting each citizen his voice in the management of affairs—equal franchises and equal liberties.

And it is the essential function of government to *preserve* and *intensify* such opportunity, to police the highways of ambition, conserve our common estate, promote initiative, umpire competition and protect it from *foul plays.*

So long as the best hands—*and heads*—may win, any shopkeeper's son may become another Morgan—any parson's youngster, another Rockefeller —any mill-drudge, another Carnegie—any chore boy, another Ford—any messenger, another Sarnoff—any salesman, another Rosenwald—any train butcher, another Edison—any blacksmith, another Vanderlip—any depot master, another Jim Hill—any clerk, another Penny—*and any homeless orphan, another Herbert Hoover.*

The coming election is called under our by-laws to *re-insure* the guar-antees under which American politics, finance and commerce have re-mained in the *captaincy of competence,* regardless of ancestry or life start.

It is called to take stock of Federal assets, review Federal stewardship and enable shareholders (or citizens) to continue the present board of na-tional directors—that is (the Republican Party)—or vote a change of man-agement.

That decision should rest with the country's *balance sheet.*

Your directors (the Republican Party) wish to report reduced debts and taxes, factories at full capacity, export trade at full tide, basic agricul-tural improvement. And the *highest* dividends of *record.*

These dividends are individual earnings in the form of wages, income and business profits.

Comparison with any period in our development will show that the country was never more *flourishing,* never more *contented,* and never more *confident.*

A vote for the Democratic Party would be a vote for *uncertainty* and *experiment* at the *high hour* of American power and affluence.

A vote for the Democratic Party would be a vote at the risk of *lower* tariff, *lower* wages, *lower* dividends, *relaxed* immigration and prohibition laws, and a general withdrawal of investment funds.

Therefore, your directors suggest it would be *unwise* to adopt the un-tried policies the Democratic Party wishes to inaugurate—policies radically different from those under which we are now so *widely* con'ent and prosper-ous.

Republican policies have established peak *outlets* for automobile and implement plants—peak *markets* for glass, steel and apparel trades—peak *prices* for beef, wool and dairy products—peak *employment* and peak con-struction—peak *wages* for labor and peak *receipts* for capital—peak *sales-records*—and peak *values* for securities.

Republican administration has filled pay envelopes and order books— filled freight cars and garages—filled savings banks and warehouses.

Republican efficiency has *cut* working hours and *raised* workers' pay, restored to railroads service, solvency and surplus, expanded and *de-mocratized* credit, lowered rural money rates, covered the continent with good roads and *strengthened the gate against foreign pauperism, products and entanglements.*

The Republican Party marches to the polls under the banners of in-creased tariff, international independence, constitutionalism, law enforce-ment, *permissable* farm relief and impartial-public service.

National Success, Sobriety and Safety Endorse

HERBERT HOOVER

for President *of* the United States

ing and closing quotations for each stock sold on the exchange, the highest and lowest prices, and the number of stocks sold that day. For his part, Meehan received a commission for each sale.

According to accounts in the *New York Times,* activity on the stock market was slow during the early days of March, 1928, when Meehan and some other financiers decided to liven it up. Pooling their resources, Meehan and his friends began bidding up Radio stock by buying and selling mainly to each other. They felt that it would only be a matter of time before the public would be attracted by this rising stock and begin buying in earnest.

Sunday, March 4, 1928; stock market news was on the first page of the *New York Times*. Over 380 thousand shares of General Motors stock had been traded the previous day. GM had opened at 139¾ ($139.75 per share) and closed at 144½. This rise of almost five dollars per share increased the value of GM stock by $88 million. On March 7 GM passed 150 and added another $100 million to its value.

Rumors abounded: GM was going into aviation; GM was going to announce a plan for sharing profits with automobile purchasers. But on March 10, all of Wall Street temporarily forgot GM, for Meehan had decided to make his move in Radio. RCA leapt upward by 12¾ points. Spectacular? It was only a prelude to an 18-point jump on March 12. Soon rumor had it that the Duponts and the Fisher brothers were in the market and buying heavily. Other stocks also felt the pressure; Westinghouse, United States Steel, and American Linseed all had large gains. The market was no longer the domain of a few wealthy financiers; the American public caught the spirit and bought recklessly.

March ended by setting new market records. For sixteen consecutive market days, 3 million or more stocks were traded. Radio reached 195, an increase of 61 points, although it never paid a single cent in dividends. Michael J. Meehan made between $5 million and $15 million. Thus, the great "bull market" (rising market) of the 1920's was launched. Although no one knew it at the time, price levels a year later would make these quotations look weak in comparison.

Buying on Margin

While the market rose rapidly, ingenious men invented or perfected new ways to make more money. Stocks too expensive to buy outright were offered on the installment plan, like cars and refrigerators. The down payment to buy stocks was called *margin*. With a margin requirement of 25 percent, a speculator could buy a $100 share of Radio for $25 (.25 × $100). He would borrow the remaining $75 from his broker. The broker, in turn, borrowed the money from banks or large corporations. Such broker's loans were often labeled "call" money, because the lender could demand or call repayment at any time. Since "call" money was backed by stocks, it was considered a perfectly safe investment in a rising market and became a popular form of loan. Some corporations preferred making these safe loans to investing in business expansion. In fact, call loans were so profitable that corporations furnished brokers with over one-half of the $6 billion lent on call.

Buying stock on the installment plan became a highly popular pastime. Interest rates for call money averaged 8 to 9 percent annually and occasionally rose to 18 or 20 percent during emergencies. Although many securities returned dividends less than 1 or 2 percent a year (Radio never paid any), rising stock values made margin purchases profitable. In March, 1928, $25 purchased $100 of Radio stock; in September, 1929, that same stock was worth $505. The growth of $25 into $500 within 18 months was a dazzling investment. Or was it perhaps a fortunate gamble?

Margin could work in reverse. If a man contracted with a broker to buy stock at $500, with a 25 percent down payment ($125) and the stock price dropped from $500 to $250, he would still owe the broker $375. Since the market value of the stock is then less than the customer's debt, the broker cannot gamble on the man or on the stock. He must demand more down payment, or margin, to cover the drop in the stock's value; otherwise, he must sell the stock, which he holds until it is paid for in full. A purchaser who fails to pay the difference between the purchase price and the current stock price is "sold out" and loses his original investment. When many margin accounts are sold out on a falling market, each such sale helps to force prices downward. Each new drop jeopardizes other margin accounts, and the result may be a serious downturn.

Leverage Lifts Stock Prices

So great was the demand for stocks during the days of the bull or rising market that new methods were devised to increase the supply. The happiest invention to fill that need was called the Investment Trust. The trust, something like today's mutual funds, was a stock-issuing corporation which invested its assets in the stocks of other corporations. The trusts had existed in England since the 1880's and served the purpose of permitting the investor to diversify his holdings. During the 1920's it became increasingly popular in America as a device to issue more securities. There were 160 trusts in existence in 1927, 186 were formed in 1928, and another 265 in 1929.

The investment trust not only satisfied a demand for stocks but also provided opportunities for realizing great profits. The trusts issued securities and used the proceeds to buy stocks in other firms which also used the proceeds to buy stocks in yet other firms. The result of these multiple investments was called leverage. A slight increase in the value of the stocks of the original company would be multiplied into a far greater increase in the value of the second company and even a greater increase in the value of the third company and so forth. The noted economist John Galbraith explains precisely how this worked:

> Consider, by way of illustration, the case of an investment trust organized in early 1929 with a capital of $150 million—a plausible size by then. Let it be assumed further, that a third of the capital was realized from the sale of bonds, a third from preferred stock, and the rest from the sale of common stock. If this $150 million were invested, and if the securities so purchased showed a normal appreciation, the portfolio value would have increased by midsummer about 50 percent. The assets would be worth $225 million. The bonds and preferred stock would still be worth only $100 million; their earnings would not have increased, and they could claim no greater share of the assets in the hypothetical event of a liquidation of the company. The remaining $125 million, therefore, would underlie the value of the common stock of the trust. The latter, in other words, would have increased in asset value from $50 million to $125 million, or by 150 percent, and as the result of an increase of only 50 percent in the value of the assets of the trust as a whole.

This was the magic of leverage, but this was not all of it. Were the common stock of the trust, which had so miraculously increased in value, held by still another trust with similar leverage, the common stock of that trust would get an increase of between 700 and 800 percent from the original 50 percent advance. And so forth.[1]

Leverage worked with happy results in many real cases. The investment trust Goldman and Sachs, for example, launched a string of subsidiary firms, two within one month, issuing $500 million worth of securities in that month and using the proceeds to buy other stocks. Through leverage, the thirteen companies in the American Founders Group expanded a $500 investment into a billion dollar enterprise by riding the rising market.

Investment trusts in this way created millions of new securities, and the public bought without hesitation. The market seemed to possess an unlimited ability to absorb new stocks. In September, 1929, $600 million worth of investment trust certificates were issued and sold, bringing a two-year total of $8 billion. One out of ten securities now were investment trusts, firms which owned or produced nothing except stocks or bonds in other companies, many taking full advantage of leverage. This was fine while the market was still rising. Few ventured a public guess about leverage's effects on a falling market.

A Few Cases of the Jitters

Despite the proven efficiency of the new money-making techniques, predictions of disaster were occasionally heard. On numerous occasions, such predictions came uncomfortably close to being right, but the ability of the market to adjust itself and its continued buoyancy in the face of the most disastrous predictions tended to discredit pessimists. Furthermore, in an age which measured wisdom in dollars, few of the gloomy prophets were wealthy. Those who soured sold out while the market was low. Bold investors learned that this was the time to buy, for good stocks could be purchased at bargain rates during declines, and the seemingly inevitable recoveries always brought increases beyond former values. Popular prophets of the day were fearless investors like Charles Mitchell, chairman of National City Bank, who made millions during declines. They advised the public to put their faith in America. Besides, the market could never really collapse with bargain hunters to preserve it by timely purchases; and investment trusts and big money interests had too much at stake to allow a crash.

The recuperative powers of the stock market were truly remarkable. In June, 1928, Bank of America stock plummeted 100 points in a single day; Radio lost 28 points and the entire market was severely shaken. An uncertain political climate (this was during the Republican convention of 1928 and candidate Hoover had expressed pessimism about the stock market) and a suspected shortage of call money (which never really materialized) contributed to a general anxiety about the market. But recovery was quick and those who sold expecting prices to go even lower cursed their faint hearts.

In December, 1928, stocks again dropped sharply, Radio lost 72 points on December 7 and closed at 297. Montgomery Ward lost 29 points; International Harvester fell 61. But the investor with faith in the market bought at these low prices, and by the year's end the market had recovered lost ground. Radio eventually climbed to 505.

Following a comparatively stable market during the first part of 1929, stocks rose to precarious heights during July, August, and September. The quotations below from the *New York Times* of September 3, 1929, compared with earlier prices, will give you a sense of the progress of the great bull market during its first 18 months.[2]

Stock	Dividends	March 3, 1928	Sept. 3, 1929
American Can	2	77	181 ⅞
American Founders		85	117
American Tel & Tel	9	179 ½	304
General Electric	5	128 ¾	396 ½
General Motors	5	139 ¾	181 ⅞*
Goldman, Sachs			110
Radio		94 ½	505*
United States Steel	7	138 ⅛	261 ¾
Westinghouse E&M	4	91 ⅝	289 ⅞
Average for 50 leading stocks		176 ¾	307

(*values adjusted to account for stock splits)

The Way Down

During the next six weeks, stocks slowly drifted down from these heights. Observers generally assign three reasons for this decline. British speculators were forced to sell their American holdings because of problems in England; new stocks were issued which the market could not absorb; and, finally, stocks were generally priced above estimated worth of real assets. By mid-October, the *New York Times* 50-stock average dropped 16 points from the September levels. There was nothing to worry about, however, according to Irving Fisher, a Yale professor and popular market expert; stocks had reached a permanently high plateau. Banker Charles Mitchell declared, "The last six weeks have done an immense amount of good by shaking down prices. . . . The market values have a sound basis in the general prosperity of our country."[3] And brokers, long accustomed to continuous recoveries, predicted another upsurge.

Black Thursday and a Blacker Tuesday

Despite these optimistic words from high sources, an unprecedented number of selling orders were reaching Wall Street. On the afternoon of Wednesday, October 23, 1929, the ticker tape did not record the last floor transaction until nearly two hours after the market closed. The *New York Times* stock index showed an 18 point loss, the worst day's loss in the exchange's history. Lights blazed on Wall Street far into the night as tired brokers tried to balance customers' accounts. All too often their clients'

The New York Times.

VOL. LXXIX...No. 26,212.   Copyright, 1929, by The New York Times Company.   NEW YORK, WEDNESDAY, OCTOBER 30, 1929.   TWO CENTS In Greater | THREE CENTS Elsewhere | FOUR CENTS Within and to-

"All the News That's Fit to Print."

THE WEATHER
Cloudy; probably rain and tomorrow; warmer tomorrow.

STOCKS COLLAPSE IN 16,410,030-SHARE DAY, BUT RALLY AT CLOSE CHEERS BROKERS; BANKERS OPTIMISTIC, TO CONTINUE AID

CLOSING RALLY VIGOROUS

Leading Issues Regain From 4 to 14 Points in 15 Minutes.

INVESTMENT TRUSTS BUY

Large Blocks Thrown on Market at Opening Start Third Break of Week.

BIG TRADERS HARDEST HIT

Bankers Believe Liquidation Now Has Run Its Course and Advise Purchases.

240 Issues Lose $15,894,818,894 in Month; Slump in Full Exchange List Vastly Larger

LEADERS SEE FEAR WANING

Point to 'Lifting Spells' in Trading as Sign of Buying Activity.

GROUP MEETS TWICE IN DAY

But Resources Are Unable to Stem Selling Tide—Lamont Reassures Investors.

HOPE SEEN IN MARGIN CUTS

Banks Reduce Requirements at 25 Per Cent—Interest in Wall St. More Cheerful.

RESERVE BOARD FINDS ACTION UNNECESSARY

Six-Hour Session Brings No Change in the New York Rediscount Rate.

U.S. STEEL TO PAY $1 EXTRA DIVIDEND

American Can Votes the Same and Raises Annual Rate From $3 to $4.

BIG GAIN IN STEEL INCOME

Earnings for Nine Months Are $15.82 a Share, Against $9.17 a Year Ago.

GRUNDY FOR CURBING 'BACKWARD STATES' ON THE TARIFF BILL

Veteran Republican Lobbyist Tells Senate Inquiry the West Needs "Silencing."

PENNSYLVANIA KNOWS BEST

"Unfortunate," He Holds, That the Constitution Gives Equal Voice to States in Senate.

BATTLES INVESTIGATORS

COALITION FIGHTING MOVE TO KILL TARIFF

Will Try to Force Through Bill, While Reed Favors Ending Session Nov. 15.

WATSON QUITTING CAPITAL

Departure for Florida Tomorrow for Health Leaves Jones as Republican Senate Leader.

KAHN REFUSES POST IN SENATE CAMPAIGN; CALLS CHOICE UNWISE

He Writes to Moses to Withhold His Name for Treasurer Due to 'Divided Reception.'

WAS RELUCTANT, HE SAYS

Recalls He Told Senator of His Stand, but Yielded as a Duty to His Party.

HOLDS VIEWS CONFIRMED

Van Opel, Rocket Flier, Weds Woman Pilot Who Advised Him

MISSING AIRLINER BROUGHT IN SAFELY

Pilot Lands Western Express Ship at Albuquerque After Being Forced Down.

WOULD NOT RISK STORM

Passengers Tell of Cold Night in Desert Ranch House as Snow Swirled Round.

Newark Man, 4 Feet 10, Says He Was Smallest in A. E. F.

margin had been exhausted, which meant they had to supply more money or lose their stock. To obtain money speculators had to sell some shares. The next day, Thursday, October 24, brought a deluge; thousands of forced-sale orders streamed in. Blocks of 10,000 and 20,000 shares were thrown on the market for whatever they might bring. So many were selling at once, to meet cash requirements, that prices dropped still lower. The further prices fell, the more cash was needed, and the more stocks had to be sold at sacrifice prices. Individual stocks plummeted 2, 3, and even 5 points between sales. Leading stocks lost 30 to 40 points within two hours. Long before the closing bell sounded, the entire market had dropped 30 points, nearly double the record loss of the previous day. More than $40 billion in paper values had disappeared.

"205 for 20,000 shares of United States Steel."

J. P. Morgan's broker, Richard Whitney, made this startling bid. Whitney could have had the stock for 193 ½, but his bid on steel and $20 million to $30 million worth of other stocks was purposely high to stabilize the market and end the panic. The daring gamble was successful. Floor traders realized that Whitney represented a pool of New York City's major bankers and that organized support had come to rescue the faltering market. The market rallied. When the tired ticker caught the final quotations, some four hours after closing, 12 million shares had changed hands, while prices regained two-thirds of the day's losses. The banker's pool had courageously checked a major collapse.

The teetering market continued recovering Friday and Saturday. Bargain hunters were purchasing solid stocks at fire-sale prices. The bankers' pool carefully unloaded most of the stocks it purchased on Thursday. The bankers could not afford to be caught if a final collapse came. Over the weekend, brokers hastily examined their clients' accounts. Many lacked margin requirements and would again be forced to sell some stocks to cover others. Monday's market abounded with "sell" orders, wiping out investors who had exhausted their margin. That day the market lost 26 points. But the worst was yet to come. The acceleration of forced selling created the panic that has caused Tuesday, October 29, 1929, to be remembered as Black Tuesday. Pandemonium on the floor of the exchange was heightened by outside traders who were watching tickers that were running four hours late and were frantically calling in sales orders. One bewildered broker was so beset by orders he could not fill that he piled them in the trash basket for safe keeping, only to find them still unfilled the next day. An enterprising messenger boy bid $1.00 for White Sewing Machine and, in the absence of other bids, bought the stock as prices were dropping out of sight.

Margin and Leverage in Reverse

Where were the market's saviours? The bankers' pool had also been selling and was unable to do more than cushion the shock as Americans unloaded their stocks. Bargain hunters were buying only when they could and dared, at prices considered ridiculously low two days before. The investment trusts suddenly found leverage working in reverse with deadly

Just as many People Employed...
Just as many Wheels Turning...
Just as many Dollars...

efficiency. While the selling price of Goldman, Sachs stocks was reduced by almost 50 percent, a subsidiary, Blue Ridge, was reduced by 70 percent. Certain holdings in the American Founders Group, designed to secure maximum leverage, dropped to mere pennies a share.

The logic of buying on margin and of leverage had pushed the market to dizzy heights. While the market was rising and as long as there was money to be made, all was well. But when the market started falling, margin accounts were soon exhausted, forcing sales at declining prices. Now leverage whipped values down still further Nearly 16.5 million shares changed hands on October 29 as industrial stocks lost an average of 43 points. Wall Street had never seen a day quite like it. It marked the end of the prosperous Twenties and the beginning of the Great Depression. Stocks continued a faltering descent to hit a low in July, 1932.

The table below suggests an epitaph for the great bull market of the Twenties: slain by margin, leverage, and panic.[4]

Stock	High price Sept. 3, 1929	Low Oct. 29, 1929	November 13, 1929	July 8, 1932
American Can	181 ⅞	110	86	31 ½
American Founders	85	66	67	½
American Tel & Tel	304	264	197 ¼	71 ¾
General Electric	396 ½	210	168 ⅛	9
General Motors	181 ⅞	33 ¼	36	56 ¾
Goldman, Sachs	110	55	32	1 ⅜
Radio	505	130	140	17 ½
United States Steel	261 ¾	166 ½	150	21 ½
Westinghouse E&M	289 ⅞	100	102 ⅝	15 ½
Average for 50 leading stocks	307	183 ½	166 ⅛	34

(American Founders and Goldman, Sachs were investment trusts)

NOTES

1. John Kenneth Galbraith, *The Great Crash* (Boston: Houghton Mifflin Company, 1961), pp. 62–63.

2. Frederick Lewis Allen, *Only Yesterday* (New York: Harper & Row, Publishers, Inc., 1931), (based in part on tables on) pp. 295, 318.

3. *Ibid.*, p. 324.

4. *Ibid.*, (based in part on table on) p. 337.

QUESTIONS

1. How did business profits, confidence, leverage, and margin contribute to the "bull" market of the 1920's?

2. Once the market collapse started, what made it so sudden and disastrous?

3. Are there any reasons to think that a stock crash was "due," or inevitable, soon after September, 1929? Explain.

SUGGESTED READING

Accounts of the market's activities and fluctuations are found in all histories of the 1920's. John Kenneth Galbraith, *The Great Crash, 1929* (Boston: Houghton Mifflin Company, 1961) shows that boundless optimism, leverage, and margin caused the debacle. A vivid and informative view of the crash is presented by Frederick Lewis Allen in *Only Yesterday* (New York: Harper & Row, Publishers, Inc., 1931). Robert Sobel provides a more scholarly treatment in *The Great Bull Market: Wall Street in the 1920's* (New York: W. W. Norton and Company, 1968).

Chapter 5

What Caused the Depression?

Introduction

Nineteen twenty-nine marked more than the end of the bull market. It signaled the end of a nine-year period of prosperity and heralded the onslaught of the Great Depression. Moreover, 1929 ended an era when the easy assumptions of laissez-faire conservatives could be considered the ultimate in economic wisdom.

To understand the Depression and the revolution in economic thinking that accompanied it, the causes must be examined. This chapter uses the hypothetical example of one man, Frank Conner, to portray these causes in personal terms. It then introduces basic economics to identify some main factors that can cause upward and downward movements in the business cycle, and concludes with some of the questions asked then and since as to what caused the Depression.

The Conners and the Depression

When the Depression began in 1929, Frank Conner owned a medium-sized printing establishment in Chicago, Illinois. Through hard work, he had built it up in the years following his return from World War I. By 1928, business profits were over $300 monthly. In addition, Mr. Conner, as president of the establishment, paid himself a healthy salary. He attributed his success to hard work and clever business practices, for he kept abreast of the times. By buying the newest labor-saving machinery, Conner was able to reduce the number of men working in his shop by 20 percent while tripling business volume. Furthermore, he had been able to establish an excellent working relationship with his union and therefore had no labor problems. Frank Conner faithfully retained the loyal and more experienced men who were working in the print shop when he bought it, and with their consent laid off the apprentice printers before they became eligible for journeyman's wages. Conner paid an average weekly wage of $40.

36

The stock market crash cost Conner $10,000 of his savings. Most of his money was in an investment trust that lost over one-half its value in the fall of 1929, and he sold a little too late. But Conner saved nearly $5,000 from this disaster and left it in a financially strong bank. Despite the crash, Conner remained optimistic about his business, for it had survived earlier business fluctuations. Besides, he did not expect a depression; he believed the fundamental business of the country was sound. Even the paper losses he absorbed during the Crash did not worry him much. Stocks were likely to rise again and Conner was planning to buy securities as soon as the market gave definite promise.

As 1930 lapsed into 1931, the Conners were still doing reasonably well. Few of Mr. Conner's old business accounts canceled their contracts, though most placed smaller orders. He let his apprentices go and put the rest of the shop on a five day, thirty-five hour week. His workers' pay decreased correspondingly. Meanwhile, Mrs. Conner cut back on her household expenses. The Conners did not eat meat every day, nor did they go to the motion pictures as often. Sundays, they still took their customary drive in the country, though the children, Dick and Louise, were not treated to ice-cream sodas. Mr. Conner did not get the new suit he had been planning to buy, and Louise had to go to the Senior prom in a gown she had made herself.

Shortly after the Christmas season, 1931, Frank Conner lost his biggest account. He had to reduce his work force to five men, and he could keep them working by running only the smaller machines. Though his firm lost money, he could not bring himself to fire the men who had worked faithfully for fourteen years. He tried renting out part of the plant's floor space to another company. No one was interested.

During 1932, Frank Conner lost heavily on his business. He threw his savings into it in the hopes that conditions would soon improve. But the upward turn never came, and the large account didn't materialize. With his firm hopelessly in debt, Conner finally sold out, using the proceeds to pay his bank loans. The Conner Print Shop was no more.

Frank Conner could not find work in Chicago after losing his business. He decided to move his family to Richmond, Iowa, where he could live rent free with his in-laws. Since they had a farm, his family would not starve, and it was possible that he could get work on the federal dam being constructed in the neighboring county. Besides, Dick and Louise could attend school in Richmond. The schools in Chicago were in serious trouble, for the teachers had not been paid in several months.

The Conners were better off than most when the Depression started and in worse straits than many when it reached bottom. Cases like Frank Conner's were ironic; business decisions that Conner and thousands of other businessmen made during the Twenties to increase their profits helped to cause or deepen the Depression, which in turn made them its unhappy victims. The following pages show why Frank Conner and millions of Americans became the captives of economic forces they had released but could not reverse.

The Flow of Income and Spending

A student of economics makes an obvious assumption: What is produced, he tells us, will eventually be bought. The relationship between producing and selling seems simple and logical. Wages and salaries provide workers with the money to buy or consume the products they have produced. Businessmen who receive this money then use it to produce more goods and pay their workers, who again have money to buy the products they have created. This circular flow of money is illustrated below.

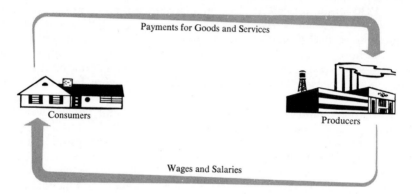

This diagram is still incomplete. While it has wages and salaries moving in one direction, it does not indicate the work done to earn them. Similarly, payments for goods and services going to the businessmen were shown without indicating a corresponding flow of products back to the consumer. The consumer must get the goods and services for which he has paid. The chart below completes these transactions.

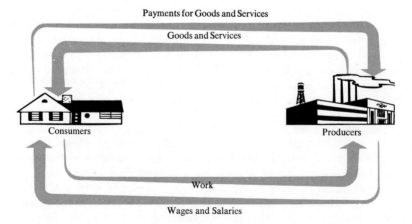

This diagram still falls short of portraying our economy as it really functions. It fails to show two extremely important economic institutions which interrupt the flow of payments. Government removes money from the income flow through taxes and returns it to the economy through expenditures. Equally important, banks hold consumer and business savings and return portions to business in the form of investments. Government and banks, then, interrupt and redirect the flow of money payments. Their activity is portrayed below as follows:

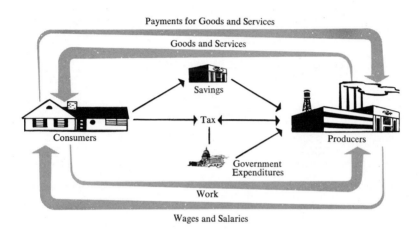

Several simple observations may be made by carefully studying the previous diagram. Money is removed from the flow of payments by (1) consumers (household) and business for saving, and (2) government in the form of taxes. We see also that money is returned to this flow through (1) investments and (2) government spending. Whether more money is removed from the expenditure flow than is returned to it will depend on (1) whether aggregate or total savings exceed aggregate or total investments, or (2) whether government taxes exceed expenditures; that is, if the budget is balanced.

Who Saves?

One may temporarily omit the flow of government expenditures in order to concentrate on the problem of saving. Most individuals have difficulty saving. Yet the record shows that people do save. Economists have discovered that people with high incomes save a greater percentage of their earnings than people with low incomes. The table on the following page shows precisely how much savings increased as income expanded during the 1920's.

What do these figures indicate? During the 1920's, 631,000 families or 2.3 percent saved two-thirds of all the money saved, and 78 percent of the families at the bottom of the income scale had practically no savings at all. What happened to the $15 billion savings held in 1929?

$1.5 billion bought real estate

$3.2 billion invested in new industries

$6.0 billion bought stocks in companies that bought stocks or bid up the value of stocks already purchased

$4.3 billion bid up value of securities already purchased or bought securities in foreign companies

In other words, a very small percentage of savings actually found its way back into investments. Most was siphoned off from the flow of payments into stocks and investment trusts, or abroad into foreign loans. Therefore, most of the savings were not returned to income flow during 1929.

SAVINGS BY FAMILIES BY INCOME GROUPS, 1929 [1]

Income group	Families (in 1000's)	% of total national income	Savings in millions	% of total national savings
Under $1000	5,899	21.5	$—2,138	—15.0
$1,000 to $1,999	10,455	38.0	801	5.0
$2,000 to $2,999	5,519	18.9	1,490	10.0
$3,000 to $4,999	3,672	13.4	2,317	16.0
$5,000 to $9,999	1,625	5.9	2,549	17.0
$10,000 and over	631	2.3	10,120	67.0
	27,474	100.0	15,139	100.0

Saving, Spending, and Investing

It is necessary to define clearly the meaning of the words save and spend. Economists identify three kinds of spending: personal consumption expenditures, i.e., the money spent by households or consumers; business spending for investment in such real assets as buildings and machines; and government spending. Business spending or investment in real assets must not be confused with business purchases of financial assets such as stocks or bonds. The latter are not business investments but merely part of the process of transferring funds from savers to businessmen who do the real investing. Since most of the money lavished on stocks in 1929 never was used to purchase tangible assets, economists do not classify the bulk of these paper transactions as investments.

Excess Saving and Fewer Purchases Mean Depression

Money was used to buy stocks in GM or RCA rather than to purchase cars and radios. People bought stocks in investment trusts rather than new houses. Farmers produced surpluses while millions went hungry. At least two different sets of reasons explain these incongruities. The illusions of quick riches through stock speculation channeled money away from legitimate investment into securities that represented no real values. Perhaps a more fundamental explanation is the maldistribution of income which put proportionately more money in the hands of people with a high propensity to save and too little money into the hands of those with a low propensity to save. Illustrative of the wage and profit structure which increased the inequities in income was the example of the Conner enterprise which expanded production and profits during the 1920's much more rapidly than wages and employment. By 1929 workers did not earn enough money to buy back the goods they produced. The savings of the rich were not channeled back into the economy by business investment. This deflationary gap was not remedied by the taxing and spending powers of the government. Quite the reverse, cuts in taxes and expenditures increased the income differential between rich and poor and accentuated the gap between production and purchasing power. Had industries lowered prices their workers might have been able to purchase more of their products, but increased concentration of production in the hands of a few firms minimized competition and prices remained artificially high. In the end Americans paid dearly for the structual defects which caused the Depression. Economists estimate the loss of production during the 1930's at about $500,000,000 billion, an amount equal to the monetary price of World War II.

The structural weaknesses of the economy are illustrated by some concrete examples, listed below:

the 36 thousand wealthiest families received as much income as the 12 million poorest

between 1923 and 1929, corporate profits rose by 62 percent, dividends by 65 percent, workers income by 11 percent

71 percent of the people lived in families whose total income was less than $2500; 42 percent earned less than $1500

between 1923 and 1929 output per man hour rose 32 percent and wages only 8 percent

the textile, shoe, and agriculture industries were depressed during the 1920's

about $4 billion was spent on purchasing foreign securities in 1929

about $7 billion in brokers' loans was lent to purchase stocks on margin

in 1929, 3.2 percent of the working force was unemployed

about 200 giant non-banking firms controlled almost half of the non-banking corporate wealth and, it was feared, conspired in many cases to keep prices artificially high.

Government policy during the 1920's contributed to the general structural deficiencies of the economy:

Mellon's tax policies saved wealthy Americans millions of dollars during the 1920's

practically no efforts were made to enforce the anti-trust laws

the U.S. Treasury carried a $750 million surplus in 1929

President Hoover resisted pressure to start building government flood control projects in the Tennessee Valley

the McNary-Haugen plan was defeated

Once the Depression started, it contributed to the general deficiencies which had caused it:

the bulk of savings diverted to stocks was wiped out as the market value of stocks listed on the New York Exchange fell from $89.5 billion in 1929 to a low of 15.5 billion in 1932

almost 25 percent of the labor force was unemployed in 1933

NOTE

1. Louis Hacker, *American Problems of Today* (New York: F. S. Crofts and Company, 1938), p. 185.

QUESTIONS

1. How does the following statement make sense in terms of the income flow charts: when savings exceed investments, production is greater than purchasing power.

2. Did Mellon's policies (see Chapter 2) contribute to savings exceeding investments? Explain.

3. How would the factors listed on pp. 41–42 help cause the Depression?

SUGGESTED READING

It is suggested that students of the Depression read pertinent sections of standard college economics texts. For further information on the causes of the Depression, see Broadus Mitchell, *Depression Decade: From New Era Through New Deal, 1929–1941* (New York: Rinehart and Company, Inc., 1947), and Lewis Kimmel, *Federal Budget and Fiscal policy 1789–1958* (Washington, D.C.: Brookings Institution, 1959). For an analysis that blames "a bankrupt Republican administration" as well as short-sighted business leaders see Arthur M. Schlesinger, Jr., *The Crisis of the Old Order, 1919–1933* (Boston: Houghton Mifflin Company, 1957).

UNIT II.
PURCHASING POWER AND THE DEPRESSION

During the 1920's, Andrew Mellon succeeded in balancing the budget, reducing taxes, and limiting federal expenditures. For eight years these policies stimulated business, helped feed the stock market, and provided an uneven prosperity. Then, in 1929, the stock market crashed and the Great Depression began.

If a depression is caused by a failure in investment and in consumer purchasing power, one would assume that the federal government should spend enough and in such a way as to make up these deficiencies when private industry cannot. President Hoover did not accept this line of thinking, for four important reasons. First, he was convinced there was nothing fundamentally wrong with the American economy; second, he thought that prosperity trickled down from the wealthy to the poor; third, he believed businessmen could revive the economy if their confidence in the government was restored, and fourth, he felt that federal spending would create deficits that would further undermine business confidence. Finally, Hoover felt it was the responsibility of local governments rather than of the federal government to help the unemployed. Federal spending, Hoover asserted, would destroy local initiative. Consequently, he concentrated on measures to revive big business and keep the banks from bankruptcy.

After three years of deepening depression, Americans elected Franklin D. Roosevelt, who believed there was something radically wrong with the economy. He believed it the responsibility of the federal government to prevent starvation, and he spent billions providing relief for the unemployed. He believed prosperity trickled up from the poor as well as down from the rich, but was not at all convinced that deficits in the federal budget were anything but a necessary evil, so he tried balancing the budget as soon as he dared.

The following chapters focus a study of the 1930's on three issues: federal spending vs. budget balancing; trickle up vs. trickle down; and local vs. national responsibility for aiding the destitute. The reader will study both sides of the controversies involving these questions to help him decide how the federal government may best end an economic collapse.

President Herbert Hoover and his family

Chapter 6
President Hoover and the Depression

Introduction

President Hoover, pledged to the normalcy policies of the 1920's, but now called upon to combat a grossly abnormal depression, broke some of the restrictions of normalcy. He enormously increased the role of the government in the economy, clinging to laissez-faire ideas, but departing from laissez-faire practice. This chapter examines Hoover's view of causes of the Depression and calls for an analysis of issues posed by his methods for restoring prosperity.

Portrait of the Depression

Perhaps it would have been possible to live through the Depression and hardly be aware of its existence. In the Hoover years, Henry Ford innocently remarked, "These are really good times, but only a few know it."[1] Few, indeed; people were affected directly all over the country.

Los Angeles: People who had their gas and electricity cut off cook by wood fires on vacant lots. Four-year-old Narcissas Sandoval, having lived on refuse, dies of starvation.

St. Louis: One thousand people camp in shacks constructed of scrap metal. Similar Hoovervilles spring up in every major city.

Pennsylvania: Unemployed miners eat wild roots and dandelions.

Kentucky: Coal miners learn to eat all weeds chewed by cows because they know these animals never eat poisonous vegetation.

Massachusetts: Anthony Prasel, father of eight, shoots himself because he can not provide for his family.

Washington, D.C.: Ten thousand World War I veterans cram themselves into a shantytown, Anacostia Flats, waiting for Congress to pay their bonuses. The Senate defeats the bill and federal troops disperse the veterans and burn their shacks.

Sioux City, Iowa: Farmers, driven to desperate measures as agricultural

45

prices reach rock bottom, camp on U.S. Highway 20 and prevent farm produce from entering town.

Unemployment mounted: 8 million in 1931; 12 million in 1932; 13 million in 1933, and some estimates put the figure as high as 17 million. An untold number worked only two or three days a week. Additional millions took cuts in wages as wage payments fell from $50 to $30 billion.

Somewhere between 1.5 to 2 million people were on the road—living in city parks, under bridges, and in caves and railroad cars—looking for work. One out of twenty were girls. Two-hundred thousand were still in their teens, or younger. In Connecticut, the Commissioner of Labor reported 100 establishments employing young girls for anywhere from 60 cents to $1.10 for a 55-hour week. National income plummeted from a high of $87.4 billion in 1929 to a low of $41.7 billion in 1932.

Herbert Hoover

It was a cruel irony which brought Herbert Hoover into the office of president on the eve of the Depression. Born in 1874, Hoover worked his way through college, labored briefly as a two and one-half dollar a day miner, and became a millionaire before reaching forty. Having succeeded in the business world, Hoover turned to government service. During World War I he distinguished himself as director of relief for war-torn Belguim, and after the war his humanitarian activites were expanded to cover all of Europe. Hoover's service won so much esteem that he was in the running for the Republican nomination in 1920. President Harding picked him to serve as Secretary of Commerce and Hoover played a major role in shaping the policies of the 1920's. His unshakable faith in laissez-faire capitalism had been fostered by his successful business career and by the miraculous performance of the American economy. In a campaign speech in 1928 Hoover expressed his confidence in America, "We are nearer today to the ideal of the abolition of poverty and fear from the lives of men and women than ever before in any land."

Hoover believed that the conservative policies of the eight years during the 1920's were responsible for the prosperity of that period. When the Depression came he did not think there was anything fundamentally wrong with the American economy. The great irony of Hoover's life was that his belief in the American system of private enterprise blinded him to the possibilities of effective governmental intervention, and his adherence to the doctrine of individualism made him incapable of dealing with mass suffering and unemployment in his own land.

Not Laissez-Faire

The United States had experienced a depression in 1893, a panic in 1907, and a brief recession in 1921–22. Each of these disruptions had corrected itself without government intervention in the operation of the economy. According to the old economic theory of business cycles, depressions were caused by high prices, overproduction, and excessive indebtedness. These imbalances were corrected when prices fell so low that people could once again buy goods. Then production would resume, prices rise, and wages increase; the upturn in purchasing and production would restore prosperity. Meanwhile, bankruptcy would bring down the excessive debt of business firms and receivers could begin operations without a high debt overhead. The government should not interfere with the downward cycle because it brings prices to realistic levels and permits purchasing and production to resume.

Hoover however rejected the extreme laissez-faire notion that Depressions must run their course without any interference from government. But he was unable to use the full power of government to stabilize production and wages because he knew it would require coercion, which he felt was destructive to personal liberty. The president therefore relied on voluntary cooperation of businessmen.

Voluntarism in Government

As Secretary of Commerce in the 1920's Herbert Hoover had encouraged self-government in business through trade associations which established standards of fair business practices, regulated wages, and ended sweatshop labor conditions. As president, Hoover relied on voluntary cooperation to maintain employment, production, and wages. In this way he thought that he could stop the competitive wage and price cuts that usually accompany a downturn in business.

On his first of many meetings, Hoover brought such industrial greats together as Henry Ford, Pierre Dupont, Alfred Sloan of General Motors, Owen Young of General Electric, Walter Teagle of Standard Oil, and Myron Taylor of United States Steel. He told these leaders of the nation's largest industries that they were not to solve their business problems by cutting wages, firing employees, and halting production. They were to continue business until the slight downturn stopped. In this way, no one need suffer from a depression.

To a surprising degree, these captains of industry agreed to follow Hoover's advice, and until the summer of 1931 they held wage rates at their prosperity levels, though employment at best was part time. The industrialists were not willing to maintain production for a nonexistent market, and to this extent Hoover's program of voluntarism failed. He could not get businessmen to produce goods where there were no buyers in sight.

The Economy is Fundamentally Sound

True to his deep-seated faith in the American system, Hoover did not blame the Depression on any basic malfunction of the American economy. The causes of the Depression, he felt, lay outside the United States. He blamed the Depression on the disruptions of world trade and credit by World War I, on revolutions in China, on the collapse of a market for cocoa in Ecuador, and on banking failures in Austria. In his last year as president, Hoover convinced himself that the Depression had all but ended. When this proved untrue, he blamed the relapse on fear and panic which he claimed was caused by president-elect Roosevelt's policies. Hoo-

Heh! Heh! The Worm Turns.

A nervously optimistic view of the situation, November, 1931.

ver did recognize that a disruption of economic activities was precipitated by the stock market crash, and that the crash was responsible for a loss of faith and confidence in the economy. Aside from this admission, he did not look for causes of the Depression within the American system of production and distribution of goods, nor did he ever acknowledge any serious economic problems during the 1920's which might have caused the Depression.

Since there was nothing fundamentally wrong with the economy, according to Hoover, much of the Depression was caused by panic and fear. Therefore, the president's job was to reassure the nation that nothing was really wrong with the country or the economy. This philosophy inspired a series of confident statements. Shortly after the stock market crash he told the nation that, "The fundamental business of the country, that is, the production and distribution of commodities, is on a sound and prosperous basis." In March, 1930, he informed the country that the Depression would be over in sixty days, and so many other administration spokesmen continued this "prosperity is just around the corner" theme while breadlines lengthened that a credibility gap developed between the administration and the nation.

Saving Business

Voluntarism and optimism failed to stem the tide of business collapse. Still unwilling to follow laissez-faire, Hoover now asked Congress at least to save the major economic institutions of the land, the banks, insurance companies, railroads, etc. Congress responded by establishing the Reconstruction Finance Corporation, and Hoover later defended this departure from laissez-faire:

> Disaster has been averted in the saving of more than 5,000 institutions and the knowledge that the adequate assistance was available to tide others over the stress. This was done not to save a few stockholders, but to save 25,000,000 of American families, every one of whose very savings and employment might have been wiped out and whose whole future would have been blighted had those institutions gone down.[1]

No Relief

While Hoover broke precedent to spend $2 billion to save banks and railroads from collapse, he was unwilling to spend any federal money for direct relief. Once the federal government accepted the responsibility of helping America's unemployed, Hoover reasoned, neighbors, communities, cities, and states that had been shouldering this burden would no longer feel obligated to help. Thus government aid would destroy the feeling of neighborly cooperation and self-help so fundamental to the American way of life. Belief in these principles rather than cruelty or indifference to suffering led Hoover to approve a measure providing $45 million to save cattle in Arkansas but oppose a $25 million grant to save Arkansas farmers. As late as May, 1932, Hoover vetoed a public works bill that would have provided thousands of jobs throughout the country.

Balance the Budget

Behind Hoover's reluctance to spend federal dollars on the unemployed lay his belief in the need to keep the budget balanced.

> . . . a deficit in the budget could only be met with more taxes and more federal bond issues. That makes balancing the budget hopeless. The country also understands that an unbalanced budget means the loss of confidence of our people in the credit and stability of the government and that the consequences are national demoralization and the loss of ten times as many jobs as would be created by this program.[2]

Trickle Down

Hoover's concern with balancing the budget, saving financial institutions, opposing relief, and restoring business confidence were part of his philosophy that revival of prosperity depended primarily on business recovery. His policies were directed at helping business. Prosperity, Hoover believed, trickles down from business men to the public at large. The major job of government, Hoover once said, "was to bring about a condition of affairs favorable to the beneficial development of private enterprise." This had also been the philosophy which had governed the policy makers of the 1920's, and which at that time was widely accepted by the American people. It is the task here to decide whether the policies which flow from this philosophy are adequate to deal with the problems of the 1930's.

It seems there wasn't any depression at all!
A skeptical view of Hoover's attempts to restore confidence.

NOTES

1. Broadus Mitchell, *Depression Decade: From the New Era Through the New Deal, 1929–41* (New York: Rinehart and Company, Inc., 1947), p. 88.
2. William Starr Myers and Walter H. Newton, *The Hoover Administration, A Documented Narrative* (New York: Charles Scribner's Sons, 1936), pp. 26–27.

QUESTIONS

1. In what ways did Hoover depart from laissez-faire?

2. What were the limitations of Hoover's approach to the problems caused by the Depression?

3. What alternatives do you see to the policies pursued by Hoover, and why do you think these policies, rather than Hoover's, deal with the causes of the Depression?

SUGGESTED READING

A short and useful analysis of Hoover's reactions to the Depression is found in Richard Hofstadter, *The American Political Tradition and the Men Who Made It* (New York: Random House, 1948, 1954). For a more lengthy and slightly more favorable analysis see Harris Warren, *Herbert Hoover and the Great Depression* (New York: Oxford University Press, 1959), and for an indictment see Arthur M. Schlesinger, Jr., *The Crisis of the Old Order, 1919–1933* (Boston: Houghton Mifflin Company, 1957). Hoover's defense is *The Memoirs of Herbert Hoover: The Great Depression, 1929–1941* (New York: The Macmillan Company, 1952).

Chapter 7
Relief for the Unemployed

Introduction

On the American frontier in the eighteenth and nineteenth centuries, neighbors helped each other build homes and clear lands for farming. They banded together for mutual protection against Indians. No one thought of calling the federal government to assist in a barn raising; these vital tasks were handled by people living in the community who knew each other's needs. During the early months of the Great Depression, local communities supplied the needs of the jobless. Neighbors helped one another; employers collected one day's wages each month for the unemployed; doctors conveniently forgot to send bills; grocers carried customers on credit; relief agencies distributed food; cities and counties increased property taxes to raise money for relief.

These local means of providing assistance were considered the strongest defense against the Depression. As the national economic crisis deepened, however, and unemployment increased to 13 million, a strong feeling developed that communities could no longer support their jobless, and that the federal government must assume the responsibility. This chapter examines this crisis and the arguments for and against using the federal government to assist the unemployed.

President Hoover Opposes Federal Relief

During World War I, Herbert Hoover had given up a lucrative job with private industry to lead America's relief efforts in war-torn Europe. Hoover brought a reputation for charity to the White House. But as president during the Depression, he did not want his government to assume the role of distributing federal funds to unemployed workers and their families. Hoover believed some very important ideals were involved and would not sacrifice the principle of self-help:

This is not an issue as to whether people shall go hungry or cold in the United States. It is solely a question of the best method by which hunger and cold shall be prevented. It is a question as to whether the American people on one hand will maintain the spirit of charity and mutual self-help through voluntary giving and the responsibility of local government as distinguished on the other hand from appropriations out of the Federal Treasury for such purposes. My own conviction is strongly that if we break down this sense of responsibility of individual generosity to individual and mutual self-help in the country in times of national difficulty and if we start appropriations of this character we have not only impaired something infinitely valuable in the life of the American people but have struck at the roots of self-government. Once this has happened it is not the cost of a few more millions but we are faced with the abyss of reliance in the future upon government charity in some form or other. The money involved is indeed the least of the costs to American ideals and American institutions.[1]

La Follette and Costigan Propose Federal Relief

In Congress, Senators Robert La Follette, Jr., and Edward P. Costigan proposed granting $375 million to assist states in aiding their unemployed. To be eligible for aid, the states had to match federal dollars with state appropriations. A survey of social workers and city officials had convinced the senators that local governments could no longer do the job. As Senator Costigan put it, "Nothing short of federal assistance, early provided and efficiently and constructively extended, can possibly satisfy the conscience and good name of America."[2]

The debate over federal unemployment assistance raged throughout the land and divided both political parties. The most articulate, knowledgeable, and influential spokesmen on the subject were assembled by La Follette before the Senate Committee on Manufacturers in 1932. A sharp cross-examination of the witnesses revealed what many thought to be a general failure of local communities to provide adequate aid. Walter Gifford, president of A.T.&T., appointed by Hoover as director of a committee on unemployment relief, seriously challenged this view.

The Breakdown of Local Relief

Senator Costigan: Mr. Lurie, please give your name to the reporter and your active connections.

Mr. Lurie: My name is H. L. Lurie, and I am director of the Bureau of Jewish Social Research. . . . I am appearing today as chairman of the subcommittee on unemployment of the American Association of Social Workers.

Senator Costigan: Please proceed in your own way.

Mr. Lurie: This statement presents a summary of the status of unemployment relief and is based upon current information received from social workers in touch with conditions in their own communities. . . . This sum-

(Wide World Photos)

Unemployed men in New York line up for food.

mary is based on information received in the last two weeks from 29 important centers of population. . . .

The general picture which these reports present is of distress growing daily more desperate, of uncertainty and of increasing fears that the communities will be unable for the rest of the year to continue the meager relief which is being offered, of the growing inadequacy of relief funds being spread thinner and thinner to cover increasing want, of an uneasy knowledge that various sections of the population are being neglected, of relief activities being discontinued as dwindling relief resources are withdrawn from support of various classes of the unemployed. . . .

The inadequacy of appropriations made in communities even in states where special state relief has been granted is also apparent in a number of reports. A state welfare officials of Pennsylvania wires that the Talbot bill, making $10,000,000 available for relief purposes in the state is a drop in the bucket, that 250,000 families are receiving relief in Pennsylvania and that anything short of $60,000,000 to $70,000,000 would not even provide food. Several cities report that no help can be expected from the state because of the state debt and the inability to raise taxes to meet the necessary expenses for established departments. In a number of communities the taxpayers have prevented the city from increasing the tax rate and are questioning whether the real estate on which taxes are imposed can carry the additional burdens which the relief programs require. . . .

Dire Conditions in American Cities

. . . Few cities are providing shoes or clothing for destitute families. No money is available for necessary medical or dental care. No payment is made for gas or electric light. . . . Relief has been continuously and gradually reduced so that whole families are getting an average of $2.39 a week relief as in New York City, with $3.00 and $4.00 and at the most $5.00 a week per family in other cities. . . .

Not only are public and private funds virtually exhausted in many communities or are likely to become exhausted before the end of the fiscal year, but the outlook that funds can be obtained for the succeeding fiscal year equal to the amounts available for the present year is quite dubious . . . One community, Chicago, pictures the situation as desperate. In another, Pittsburgh, the outlook [is] "quite black." Another, Syracuse, reports that donors are in a complete state of panic because incomes are reduced, and are seriously decreasing subscriptions [for charities]. In a third community, Philadelphia, where the municipal administration is attempting to balance its budget with the tax funds in sight, there has been a revolt of taxpayers and determined opposition of taxpayers' organizations to increasing relief appropriations which can only be carried by an increase in the tax rate of real estate. . . .

Lurie Advises Federal Aid

Senator Costigan: Thank you, Mr. Lurie. Have you ever reached a conclusion as to the need, if any, for federal aid to the states in view of the conditions such as you have described?

Mr. Lurie: It seems to me that a federal program was required at least as far back as two years ago and that the longer the federal program is delayed the more desperate conditions will become.[3]

A State Official Gives Evidence of Neighborly Help

Mr. Murphy: The next witness will be Mrs. Tyson, the deputy secretary of welfare in Pennsylvania.

Mrs. Tyson: I will give first a general statement in regard to the entire state . . .

Pennsylvania is facing an economic and social crisis so acute, so devastating in its effect on family life, as to beggar description. In January [1932], 1,001,094 of the able-bodied workers of the state were totally unemployed. This means at least 3,000,000 people, a third of the population of the state, are entirely without income from their wage earners.

Pennsylvania is as yet poorly equipped with social machinery to meet this tremendous crisis. The poor boards, which constitute the only state-wide machinery for family relief, are inadequately supplied with funds and with staff workers to carry a burden that in many counties is ten times as great as in normal times. Some of the large industries have made various types of arrangements to carry their former employees. Family welfare associations, church groups, and other private agencies have rallied to meet the need. Physicians have made a generous contribution of free medical care which is of the greatest value, but which impairs their own economic security. The school teachers in many places are giving regularly from their modest families to keep children provided with shoes, clothing, and even food, in order that they may attend school. The amount of neighborly help through which families share their meager resources with more needy relatives and friends is beyond calculation.

The State Department of Welfare has faced a constantly increasing burden of work. . . .[4]

Philadelphians Without Assistance

Mr. Murphy: The next witness is Mr. Karl de Schweinitz, who is executive secretary of the Community Council of Philadelphia, and also secretary of the committee on unemployment relief.

Mr. de Schweinitz: When I appeared before the subcommittee of the Committee on Manufacturers last December, I stated that there were 238,000 persons out of work in Philadelphia. . . . There are now 298,000 persons out of work. Today 55,000 families are receiving relief. In December our per family grant was $4.39 per week per family. It is now $4.23 per family. Of this $4.23 per family, about $3.93 is an allowance for food. This is about two-thirds of the amount needed to provide a health-maintaining diet.

When I was here in December you asked me how long our funds would last. I said that I thought they would last into May. They lasted only until April 11. We are now using funds secured through the Talbot bill, which already has been referred to. We hope that the money will carry us some time into the latter part of June.

Senator Wagner: What will you do then?

Mr. de Schweinitz: I do not know. We are trying to induce the state legislature to hold a special session. That is our only hope. . . .

I want to tell you about an experience we had in Philadelphia when our private funds were exhausted and before public funds became available.

On April 11 we mailed to families the last food order which they received from private funds. It was not until April 22 that the giving of aid to families from public funds began, so there was a period of eleven days when many families received nothing. We have received reports from workers as to how these families managed. . . .

One woman said she borrowed fifty cents from a friend and bought stale bread for three and one-half cents per loaf, and that is all they had for eleven days except for one or two meals.

Here is a family of a pregnant mother and three children. They had only two meals a day and managed by having breakfast about 11 o'clock in the morning and then advancing the time of their evening meal. Breakfast consisted of cocoa, and bread and butter; the evening meal of canned soup.

Senator Costigan: Are the cases you are citing typical or extreme?

Mr. de Schweinitz: They are typical. . . .

Another family did not have food for two days. Then the husband went out and gathered dandelions and the family lived on them.

Here is another family which for two days and a half went without food.

Still another family thinking to get as much as possible with their last food order bought potatoes and for eleven days lived only on them. [5]

(Wide World Photos)

Homeless men in a makeshift shelter suffer through the New York winter.

A Revolution is Brewing

Senator La Follette (Chairman): Mr. McGrady, please give your name and connections to the reporter.

Mr. McGrady: I represent the American Federation of Labor. I might say, Senator, that it was not our intention to be represented here today. The leaders of the trade-union movement in this country have lost their patience after coming down here repeatedly to appear at the various committees in their hearings and to appeal to the committees repeatedly to do something to stop millions of our people from starving, only to be met with utter indifference on the part of the administration and leaders of the Congress. . . .

In our meeting halls—we know this to be a fact—in our meeting halls in our 29,000 centers in this country where they (union members) meet every two weeks or once a month . . . 70 percent of the time of those meetings is taken up in denouncing those who could and will not give relief.

The leaders of our organizations have been preaching patience. We have gone back so many times to these workers asking them to wait and be patient, that the administration or the Congress or the states would do something, maybe industry itself might be able to do something, and we urged them to do nothing drastic, but I say to you gentlemen, advisedly, that if something is not done and starvation is going to continue and perhaps increase, the doors to revolt in this country are going to be thrown open and the leaders

(Wide World Photos)

**Thousands of men apply for pick and shovel jobs in Newark–How many
of them would have wanted such work a few years before?**

of this government ought to know it and they ought to do something besides
crying to the world that the most important thing to be done in this country
is to balance the budget. There are another two B's besides balancing the
budget, and that is to provide bread and butter. We want that bread and
butter through work, but if we are not going to get it through work, gentlemen, the American people in this country are going to get it anyhow and they
have pretty nearly reached the end of their patience.[6]

Unemployment Relief Director Doubts Need
of Federal Aid

Senator La Follette: As a result of [your] survey, do you know how many
persons are receiving aid?

Mr. Gifford: No, it would take months to get that information.

Senator La Follette: Do you know what the standards of assistance are that
are being provided in the several states?

Mr. Gifford: They differ almost in every locality, and necessarily so. I
think the standard of aid given in some cities in the Northeast would be a
better standard than some people in other directions have enjoyed in most
prosperous times.[7]

Senator Costigan: Could you give us your estimate of how many in New
York are in need?

Mr. Gifford: No, I could not.

Senator Costigan: Can you make an estimate for Illinois where we were advised the other day there are approximately 1,100,000 unemployed?

Mr. Gifford: I could not do that.

Senator Costigan: Is your information similarly indefinite with respect to the rest of the country?

Mr. Gifford: Yes, sir.[8]

Senator Costigan: If you cannot give us any information concerning the standards of relief which are being provided in the communities will you tell us what, in your judgement, is an adequate standard of relief?

Mr. Gifford: Well, it would vary in different cities. I can tell you about New York City because I happen to know about that. For a family, $15 a week. . . .

Senator Costigan: Take Philadelphia: Do you think that the standards of relief in Philadelphia are adequate?

Mr. Gifford: I could not answer that. . . .

Senator Costigan: Do you think we should be concerned that people in Philadelphia are not receiving adequate relief?

Mr. Gifford: Of course, we are all concerned, as human beings, on that subject, but whether we should be concerned in the federal government officially with it, unless it is so bad it is obviously scandalous and even then we would not be obliged to be concerned. . . .[9] May I read a very short statement on that?[10]

Senator Costigan: Surely.

Local Communities Providing Adequate Relief

Mr. Gifford: . . . A check of the unemployment relief situation by states which I have just made, . . . indicates that, subject to action by legislatures in possibly some four or five instances, each state will care for its own who must have help this winter.

. . . Local governments as a whole have probably always made the largest money contribution. The private agencies cooperating with them have, in general, taken care of the problems which the governmental agencies . . . can not so well handle.

These private and public funds, however, do not include what is called "invisible" relief. I refer to the cash aid and the board and lodging extended to relatives, friends, and neighbors; to the aid given by religious, fraternal, labor, and other organizations; to the voluntary or involuntary remission of debts by merchant, landlords, and others; and to the aid . . . extended by business concerns to former employees. . . . It seems clear that if the total of this invisible relief, which is obviously incalculable, were known it would be found that the private contributions very greatly exceed the public. . . .

Danger of Federal Assistance

Should such community and state responsibility be lessened by federal aid, the sincere and wholehearted efforts of the hundreds of thousands of volunteers engaged both in raising and administering relief funds would doubtless be materially lessened. Individuals would tend to withdraw much of the invisible aid they are now giving; private funds raised by popular subscription would become less; efforts to spread work and to provide work that would not be done except for the emergency would be lessened; business organizations would tend to do less for former employees. Communities, counties, and states undoubtedly would appropriate less public moneys. The net result might well be that the unemployed who are in need would be worse instead of better off.[11]

Senator Costigan: Referring for a moment to your philosophy, do you think it is a sound program to conscript Americans in war and to disregard their urgent physical need for food in times of peace? I speak now nationally.

Mr. Gifford: I should think the situation is a little different.

Senator Costigan: You regard it as entirely proper to take the sons of this country and send them into war, into battle, and to ignore, nationally speaking, the needs of those same individuals in times of peace?

Mr. Gifford: No; what I mean is that the making of war, obviously, is a national function and must be. I do not think the needs of the people should be ignored—not for one minute. The only question I am discussing is that in my view they should be left to the local cities and communities to take care of and not the federal government.

Senator Costigan: Are we not citizens of the nation as well as of the several states?

Mr. Gifford: Yes, sir.

Senator Costigan: Does the Constitution of the United States not contemplate the general welfare fully as much as any state constitution?

Mr. Gifford: I am not a lawyer, and I might have to check that up; while I am, of course, perfectly willing to answer these questions, what I really had in mind, Senator, is what I think is the practical way to do the best job, and that is all.[12]

Senator Costigan: How are you able to conclude as to the needs of a state in view of your advice to this committee that you do not know those needs?

Mr. Gifford: I am relying on the reports of our state representatives which are, presumably, based on information from the state committees appointed by the governors, which have studied the needs of the states.

Senator Costigan: The reports made by those who look at life as optimistically as you do, Mr. Gifford?

Mr. Gifford: I hope you are not criticizing me for looking at life optimistically.[13]

The Problem Summarized

What, then, was the proper function of the federal government? President Hoover and his relief director, Mr. Gifford, were certain that local and neighborly assistance, which was protecting millions, would be replaced by a dependence on federal charity once the government started making handouts. They thought it would destroy the moral fiber of the American people, who in any future crisis would turn to the government for help instead of relying on themselves and their neighbors.

But Karl de Schweinitz and others reported great suffering in cities and a breakdown in relief. Mr. McGrady even predicted a revolution unless the federal government started thinking of providing bread and butter rather than of balancing the budget.

The decision to give federal aid during a depression would be irreversible. Neighbors would indeed be less likely to come to each other's aid once federal responsibility was acknowledged. What then should be done and why?

NOTES

1. Ray Wilbur and Arthur Hyde, *The Hoover Policies* (New York: Charles Scribner's Sons, 1937), p. 375.

2. Arthur M. Schlesinger, Jr., *The Crisis of the Old Order, 1919–1933* (Boston: Houghton Mifflin Company, 1957), p. 226.

3. United States Congress, Senate, Committee on Manufacturers, *Federal Cooperation in Unemployment Relief,* hearings before subcommittee, 72nd Congress, 1st Session, on S. 4592, May 9, 1932 (Washington, D.C.: U.S. Government Printing Office, 1932), pp. 9–13.

4. *Ibid.,* pp. 14–15.

5. *Ibid.,* pp. 20–22.

6. *Ibid.,* pp. 35–37.

7. United States Congress, Senate, Committee on Manufacturers, *Unemployment Relief,* hearings before subcommittee, 72nd Congress, 1st Session, on S. 174 and S. 262, December 28, 1931–January 9, 1932 (Washington, D.C.: U.S. Government Printing Office, 1932), p. 314.

8. *Ibid.,* p. 320.

9. *Ibid.,* p. 316.

10. *Ibid.,* p. 312.

11. *Ibid.,* p. 313.

12. *Ibid.,* p. 320.

13. *Ibid.,* p. 326.

QUESTIONS

1. Do you agree with President Hoover that federal charity would destroy the feeling of local responsibility? Why?

2. What does the Senate testimony reveal about the local communities' ability to support their unemployed?

3. How much, if any, aid should the unemployed receive? Should they get enough to buy food? to pay the rent? to pay doctor's bills? to buy clothes? to keep their automobiles?

4. Should the federal government provide jobs instead of relief?

SUGGESTED READING

The condition of the unemployed is poignantly portrayed in accounts collected by Milton Metzer in *Brother Can You Spare a Dime: The Great Depression, 1929–1933* (New York: Alfred A. Knopf, 1969). David A. Shannon, ed., *The Great Depression* (New York: Prentice-Hall, 1960) contains fifty-six documentary accounts of the Depression grouped by topics. A moving contemporary account is Mauritz A. Hallgren. *Seeds of Revolt* (New York: Alfred A. Knopf, 1933). Irving Bernstein, *The Lean Years* (Boston: Houghton Mifflin Company, 1960) is an excellent social history of the 1930's.

Chapter 8
Hoover, Roosevelt, and the Banking Panic

Introduction

Perhaps the government and the economy were never closer to the brink of disaster than on March 4, 1933. Unemployment had reached 13 million. Industry and agriculture were at a standstill. During the previous weeks men and women had been racing to the nation's banks in order to withdraw their money. In twenty-one states all the banks were already closed by orders of the governors in an effort to forestall bankruptcy. Franklin D. Roosevelt, himself partially paralyzed by polio, prepared to deliver his inaugural address to a nation paralyzed by disaster and numbed by fear. This chapter tells the story of the banking crisis and permits the reader to evaluate the economic ideas and political methods of two presidents, Hoover and Roosevelt, in dealing with it.

The Banking Crisis

Business at the First National Bank of Melrose was proceeding as usual when the bank was suddenly invaded by a troop of state examiners. Customers were quietly ushered out, the bank's doors were quickly closed and bolted. A small sign hung on the plate glass door—the bank was to remain closed till further notice. Depositors could not withdraw their money; no checks from the First National would be honored. Rumors started that Mr. Johnson, the bank's president, had retired to Canada with his blonde secretary, but nobody was certain.

Mrs. Gearman sobbed and screamed without restraint in front of the First National. The closed bank contained her account of $2000 from her husband's insurance, and the $963 she had saved from making rag rugs over a twenty-five year period. The other depositors received only 31 percent of their savings when the bank settled its accounts several months later, but grief had driven Mrs. Gearman to a complete breakdown and into the insane asylum.

A Weak Banking System

No bank keeps its deposits stored in its vaults; it invests them in mortgages, car loans, government bonds, and the like. During the 1920's many banks bought speculative stocks. As the cash kept on hand forms only a small percentage of a bank's total liabilities, no bank can hold off a sudden rush for withdrawals by frightened depositors. Nearly 7000 banks failed between 1921 and 1930 and more than 5000 failed between 1929 and 1932. Failures of the worst banks caused panics that overran and swamped sound banks.

But panic was only one reason for bank failures. A Senate investigation of banks in 1932 made sensational exposures. Hoover had favored the Senate investigation, and years later he concluded that banks had been "feeble," "badly organized," and "the weakest link in our whole economic system." He did not say this in 1932, but Roosevelt did. Roosevelt called for federal regulation of stock exchanges and banks and declared that they and all corporations issuing stocks must be held, by federal law, to "truth-telling" about every stock they sold. After the elections, Congress met for its final session, and Hoover wondered whether he should ask for three new laws: a bank law; a grant of authority by which he could stop gold hoarding and gold exports; and a law for federal guarantee of bank deposits. But he decided against action, unsure about bank reform and doubtful about constitutional power to deal with the flow of gold or with a run on bank deposits.

The Banks on the Brink

On the verge of collapse in February, 1933, Michigan's largest bank, the Union Guardian Trust, appealed to the Reconstruction Finance Corporation for a $50 million loan. But the RFC was not empowered to lend more money than the bank was worth. To save the Guardian, Hoover sent two emissaries, who appealed to its largest depositor, Henry Ford. The auto king saw no reason why he, "the largest individual taxpayer in the country," should bail the government out of its loan to banks."

To save this bank and the hundreds of other Michigan banks that had lent money to the Guardian, Michigan's governor closed all banks in the state on February 14, 1933. This bank holiday, as the closing was called, triggered a run on thousands of the nation's banks. More than $900 million was withdrawn during the month of February; another $800 million in the first four days of March. One-hundred and sixty million dollars in gold was exported to foreign countries in February, and three-fourths as much in the first four days of March.

Hoover Assesses Blame

After he left office Hoover blamed Democrats for causing a new downturn in business. He claimed his administration had stimulated an upturn toward recovery, visible by July, 1932. According to Hoover's later interpretation, this recovery ended soon after the election of Roosevelt in November and was caused by businessmen's fear that the new president

(Wide World Photos)

1931–Waiting for the bank to open—it didn't.

would not balance the budget and would not protect the gold standard. Earlier, in his campaign speeches, Hoover presented the argument that Roosevelt was undermining business confidence. His final strategy in the last days before the elections was to inject fear into the minds of voters— fear that Roosevelt's policies would have terrible economic consequences. In spite of Hoover's warnings Roosevelt won the elections, carrying forty-two states to Hoover's six.

Hoover still would hold office for three months and would have the responsibility of dealing with the bank crisis. He sought for a way to restore the business confidence that he thought was the key to recovery. Privately, he felt that President-elect Roosevelt was responsible for the panic of bank depositors: "What were they [the bank depositors] afraid of? Surely not an outgoing administration with but a few days to run. Certainly not of the foreign countries, for they were steadily recovering. It was fear of the incoming administration.[1]

Roosevelt was known to be thinking of increasing the supply of money, which would inflate prices. He was, Hoover thought, bound to destroy government credit by unbalancing the budget and running unprecedented deficits. Fear of such reckless policies, reasoned Hoover, caused the runs on the banks. Hence the "knowing" depositors, in order to protect their savings, "bought foreign currencies, or securities—that is exported their capital. Other knowing ones bought real estate, and still others bought gold bullion and secreted [hid] it; less knowing ones drew gold coin; still less-knowing ones drew currency from the banks under their belief in the assurance printed upon its face that it was redeemable in gold."[2]

Hoover Asks Roosevelt for Help

Three days after the Michigan bank crisis, Roosevelt was a guest at the annual jamboree in which New York reporters put on political skits. A Secret Service messenger slipped in and handed Roosevelt a confidential letter in President Hoover's own handwriting. "Mr dear Mr. President-elect" the letter began:

> A most critical situation has arisen. . . . There is a steady degenerating confidence in the future which has reached the height of general alarm. I am convinced that a very early statement by you . . . would serve greatly to restore confidence . . . It would steady the country greatly if there could be prompt assurances that there would be no tampering or inflation of the currency; that the budget would be unquestionably balanced, even if further taxation is necessary; that the Government credit will be maintained by refusal to exhaust it by the issue of securities.[3]

Roosevelt read the letter, passed it under the table to Raymond Moley, one of his confidential advisors, and stayed through the performance, enjoying the reporters' banter. At the end, instead of rushing home to consider the message, he lingered to autograph programs and joke with friends.

Back at his house, Roosevelt studied the Hoover letter. He and his advisors concluded that Hoover was asking too much and that he was wrong in his reasoning. Hoover was asking a pledge to carry on his policies instead of the Roosevelt policies. Roosevelt reasoned that depositors were running to the banks not because they distrusted his policies but because they distrusted the banks. No high-sounding talk of balanced budgets would restore their confidence in the banks. Consequently, Roosevelt replied, "I am equally concerned with you in regard to the gravity of the present banking situation—but my thought is that it is so very deep-seated that the fire is bound to spread in spite of anything that is done by way of mere statements."[4] And then, apparently because of his secretary's oversight, Roosevelt's reply was not sent to Hoover until eleven days later.

Panic Deepens

As the day of Roosevelt's inauguration drew near, the bank panic grew ominous. Roosevelt conferred with private bankers, Treasury officials, congressional leaders, and the professional economists who served as his advisors. He seemed unperturbed. Hoover, still saddled with the responsibility, was thoroughly alarmed. His position was difficult, because he could not be certain of Roosevelt's support for corrective measures. The two men met at the White House on March 3. Emergency measures were mentioned again but Roosevelt refused to commit himself. In actuality, his confidential advisors, arriving in Washington, had in their suitcases the drafts of a series of drastic measures that Roosevelt planned to put into action. The run on the banks in the first four days of March went beyond anything ever seen before. The flight of gold abroad rose to $30 million a day; frantic depositors emptied banks of their last cash reserves; by March 4 the governors of twenty-one states had closed the banks. The country's financial structure was collapsing.

Roosevelt Speaks

Saturday, March 4, was cloudy and chilly, but 100 thousand people came to witness the inauguration of their new president. They cheered in a subdued manner as the presidential limousine passed by. Roosevelt waved in response; Hoover, knowing the applause was not for him, remained glum and silent. He hardly uttered a word during the entire ride from the White House to the Capitol steps.

The vast audience in Washington and the millions listening to their radios awaited words of deliverance from their untried leader. Roosevelt did not offer soothing words to restore business confidence; he painted a dark picture. But he called for action:

> . . . This great nation will endure as it has endured, will revive and will prosper. So first of all, let me assert my firm belief that the only thing we have to fear is fear itself—nameless, unreasoning, unjustified terror which paralyzes needed efforts to convert retreat into advance . . . Values have shrunken to fantastic levels . . . government of all kinds is faced by serious curtailment of income; the means of exchange are frozen in the currents of trade; the withered leaves of industrial enterprise lie on every side; farmers find no markets for their produce; the savings of many years in thousands of families are gone. . . . Only a foolish optimist can deny the dark realities of the moment. Yet our distress comes from no failure of substance. . . . The people of the United States have not failed. In their need they have registered a mandate that they want direct, vigorous action. . . . They have made me the present instrument of their wishes. In the spirit of the gift I take it.[5]

Roosevelt Reopens the Banks

Roosevelt fulfilled his promise of action. In his office early the next morning he found Hoover's aides had taken pencils and paper with them. Even the buzzer to summon his secretary was disconnected. For a moment paralysis in the President's office symbolized the paralysis of the nation. But a hearty shout brought the presidential secretary running. That day Roosevelt summoned Congress for an immediate special session. Thus began the famous "100 days," which saw more important federal legislation enacted than any similar period. On Monday, March 6, the new president proclaimed a bank holiday, closing all of the nation's banks for four days and temporarily suspending exports of gold and silver. On Thursday, Congress met and passed Roosevelt's emergency banking legislation, sight unseen. It retroactively affirmed the president's authority to close the banks and provided for reopening those judged sound. Meanwhile, Treasury and Federal Reserve officials feverishly reviewed the assets and liabilities of all banks. On Friday, a presidential proclamation gave the Secretary of the Treasury authority to reopen solvent institutions; Saturday, Roosevelt announced how these banks would be opened. And finally, on Sunday, he addressed the nation in the first of his famous "fireside" chats. From his studio in the White House, the president explained his actions of the previous week and appealed to all Americans to take money out of their mattresses and sugar bowls and return it to the banks; the government would see to it that their money would be safe. By Wednesday, March 15, as banks began reopening, $370 million in gold coin and gold certificates was returned ($50 million more than had been withdrawn since the first of the year). Before the end of June more than $2 billion was safely back in vaults.

Further legislation established the Federal Deposit Insurance Corporation, which insured bank accounts up to $5 thousand. Fewer banks failed during the remainder of the Depression than during any one year of the 1920's.

Hoover's predictions that Roosevelt would try currency inflation were well founded. Using the authority granted under the Thomas Amendment, Roosevelt embarked on a policy of buying gold. This would have the effect of forcing up the value of gold and forcing down the value of the dollar. His purpose was twofold. First he wanted to create inflation which would increase prices for agricultural products sold in foreign markets and help debtors pay their obligations. He called this "reflation" because he hoped to re-establish the 1929 or pre-Depression price level. The second purpose of gold buying was to forestall the Congressmen who wanted even more inflation and were prepared to force it on the country in the form of paper money not backed by gold. By 1934, the political agitation for inflation died down, and Roosevelt fixed the gold content of the dollar at 59.06 percent of its old value, or at $35 an ounce, the price it maintains today. His gold policy was only partially successful; little inflation resulted from devaluing dollars and devaluation did not noticeably stimulate the economy. However, it also did little harm.

Hoover Still Dissatisfied

The extraordinary emergency actions on money and banking enraged ex-President Hoover, who had always suspected Roosevelt's motives. The quick end to the bank crisis strengthened Hoover's conviction that "the whole panic was simply an induced hysteria among bank depositors," which he felt Roosevelt could have avoided with only ten reassuring words in January or February. Hoover felt that Roosevelt wanted the panic. Why? First, to take credit for saving the nation, and second, so he could be granted those executive powers necessary to carry out programs which, as Hoover saw it, were destructive of American ideals and principles.

NOTES

1. Herbert Hoover, *The Memoirs of Herbert Hoover: The Great Depression, 1929-1941* (New York: The Macmillan Company, 1952), pp. 215-216.
2. William Starr Myers and Walter H. Newton, *The Hoover Administration, A Documented Narrative* (New York: Charles Scribner's Sons, 1936), p. 331.
3. *Ibid.,* pp. 338-340.
4. *Ibid.,* p. 345.
5. Franklin D. Roosevelt, *The Public Papers and Addresses of Franklin D. Roosevelt,* ed. Samuel I. Rosenman, vol. II (New York: Random House, 1938), pp. 11, 15-16.

QUESTIONS

1. How did Hoover and Roosevelt explain the banking panic? Who was more nearly correct?

2. Should Roosevelt have given the nation the reassurance Hoover felt was necessary?

3. Why was Roosevelt able to end the banking crisis and Hoover unable to? Consider the personal and political factors as well as the economic.

SUGGESTED READING

Lawrence Sullivan argues the case that Roosevelt's "ambitious opportunism" was responsible for the banking crisis in *Prelude to Panic* (Washington, D.C.: Statesman Press, 1936). Herbert Feis is sympathetic to the incoming Roosevelt administration in *Characters in Crisis* (Boston: Little, Brown and Company, 1966). Also see Arthur M. Schlesinger, Jr., *The Crisis of the Old Order, 1919-1933* (Boston: Houghton Mifflin Company, 1957) and Harris Warren, *Herbert Hoover and the Great Depression* (New York: Oxford University Press, 1959).

Chapter 9
The Works Progress Administration

Introduction

When pledging a "new deal" to the American people, President Roosevelt promised work and other aid for the jobless. His efforts to give direct assistance and work relief were among the most controversial programs of his entire administration. Of the numerous programs designed to aid the unemployed, the Works Progress Administration, (WPA) was by far the largest. During the eight hectic years of its existence, the WPA spent over $11 billion, hired more than 8 million workers, and provided relief for an estimated 30 million people, roughly one-fourth of the nation. It became one of the most praised and most criticized of all the New Deal agencies.

The two charges most frequently levied against the WPA were inefficiency and politics. The word "boondoggling" was coined to describe useless projects completed under government supervision; private industry, it was claimed, could do work far more efficiently and not cost the taxpayer any of his hard-earned dollars. Government funds, critics also charged, were used to reward Democrats at the expense of Republicans.

The major part of this chapter examines the charge of inefficiency; careful consideration of this criticism is helpful today when Uncle Sam again is being called upon to provide work for jobless men and women, particularly in city slums where the unemployment rate is often over 10 percent.

From FERA to CWA

Harry Hopkins combined the tough exterior of a professional gambler with a social worker's concern for humanity. His detailed knowledge of his field and his irreverent manner won him Roosevelt's respect, and in May, 1933, the president appointed Hopkins to head the Federal Emergency Relief Administration. Hopkins's agency was given $500 million to spend on food, clothing, cash, and medical care for 4 million people. Working with local and state agencies, Hopkins began dispensing money immediately.

Meanwhile, Congress, worried about giving money away, authorized establishing another agency, the Public Works Administration, to build dams, highways, bridges, and other useful projects. To head the PWA Roosevelt chose the honest and self-righteous Harold Ickes, who personally checked into every penny his department spent.

While Hopkins's FERA was distributing aid and Ickes was carefully scrutinizing plans for each PWA project, more than 13 million Americans still faced a jobless winter in 1933. In response to protest marches of the unemployed, Congress again took action and created yet another agency, the Civilian Works Administration. Roosevelt transferred Hopkins to the CWA where he started the flow of relief money his first day in office. CWA's purpose was providing work, and Hopkins had 4 million on the payroll by January, 1934. To keep their jobs going, some workers were required to dig ditches deeper than necessary, others broke rocks with sledgehammers though machines were available. Hopkins succceeded in his prime objectives by getting millions through the winter and pouring $1 billion into empty pockets. Meanwhile, CWA workers built or repaired over 255 thousand miles of roads, enough to span the world thirty times, and this represented scarcely one-third of their accomplishments. But by the spring of 1934, with the winter emergency ending, Congress disbanded the CWA. It was hoped that its workers would be employed by private industry, but few were. Accordingly, Roosevelt devised a permanent program to care for the unemployed.

On January 5, 1935, Franklin Roosevelt asked Congress for an awesome sum, nearly $5 billion, to help only the unemployed, not the "unemployables" (those unable to work because of physical handicaps or age). Since the Depression was national in scope, finding jobs for able-bodied workers was held a national responsibility. Disabled men and women had always been the responsibility of the community or state in which they lived.

Congressional leaders frowned at Roosevelt's request for money to help the unemployed. Liberals complained about returning unemployables to the states, since thirteen states offered no established relief programs. Conservatives shouted that $5 billion was just "too damn expensive." Republicans were shocked that Roosevelt failed to provide detailed information on how the money would be spent. The bill should be reworded, Republican Senator Arthur Vandenberg complained, to read:

> Section 1. Congress hereby appropriates $4,880,000,000 to the President to use as he pleases. Section 2. Anybody who does not like it is fined $1,000.[1]

But Roosevelt's bill was passed in April, 1935, and the Works Progress Administration came into being.

Both Harry Hopkins and Harold Ickes longed to head the new $4.8 billion agency. Hopkins would spend the money quickly to create as many jobs as possible, as he had under CWA. Ickes, on the other hand, still favored the slow process of building massive public works, as under the previous PWA. Here lay the basis for a vivid conflict of personalities. Ickes is "stubborn and righteous," Hopkins confided to his diary. "He is a great resigner—anything doesn't go his way he threatens to quit. He bores me."[2] The President favored Hopkins's proposal of small projects employing as many people as possible, and Ickes accepted defeat bitterly.

> It is becoming ever clearer that Hopkins is dominating this program and this domination will mean thousands of inconsequential make-believe projects in all parts of the country.[3]

Ickes' Public Works Administration continued to do much building, but for better or for worse, Hopkins got the bulk of the money, and his philosophy dominated the administration's employment program.

The WPA in Operation

WPA's object was to provide work on useful public projects. It was not to interfere with private industry, and it should spend more for wages than for equipment. WPA paid from $5 to $19 with a weekly average of $13. Projects were initiated by local residents, in the following manner:

In the town of Plainville, U.S.A., twenty carpenters and seventy unskilled workers are unemployed. Town officials first draw a list of projects and then meet with WPA representatives. Paving Route 66 leading into Plainville might employ sixty unskilled workers and five carpenters. Building a grandstand for the football field might employ ten unskilled workers and fifteen carpenters. WPA officials then check the plan carefully before approving it. Now the federal government can pay Plainville's unemployed to work on these projects, but Plainville must supply materials: lumber for the grandstand, gravel for the road, hammers, shovels, etc. The local government must pay at least 20 percent of the total costs for each project, and the federal government pays the remaining 80 percent.

Accomplishments of the WPA

From May, 1935, to June, 1943, the WPA spent $11 billion, completing over 250 thousand different projects ranging from ". . . the construction of highways to the extermination of rats; from the building of stadiums to the stuffing of birds; from the improvement of airplane landing fields to the making of Braille books; from the building of over a million . . . privies to the playing of the world's great symphonies . . ."[4]

The WPA built or improved enough roads to circle the world twenty-four times; 700 miles of bridges and viaducts were built or repaired. Ten new buildings were constructed with WPA funds for every county in the country; another 80 thousand buildings were repaired. More than 1.5 million illiterate men and women were taught to read and write.

Criticisms of the WPA

Not everyone liked the WPA; a poll showed that 23 percent of all Americans thought it the "worst" of all New Deal programs. Budget balancers feared that government money was being wasted. Unions and industry complained of competition with regular business, while the jobless pro-

Better let that guy go!   *(The New York Times)*

Critics of WPA charged that political motives determined where projects went and who was employed.

tested low government wages and an inadequate supply of WPA jobs. Republicans complained that government jobs were used to buy votes and conservatives feared socialism. Poking fun at WPA workers became a national pastime.

Most of the complaints voiced fell into one of two categories:

1. Inefficiency of the WPA worker.
2. Political misuse of WPA funds to buy votes.

Some of the major complaints made in testimony before congressional committees are presented below. Unfortunately, this testimony can represent only a small fraction of thousands of pages dealing with some 250 thousand separate projects.

Efficiency and the WPA

Critics of the WPA, as we have seen, used the word *boondoggling* to describe its activities. It would have been far cheaper, it was argued, to give relief to the unemployed than spend money on useless projects. Private industry, made more efficient by the profit motive, would have done better work for less.

Hundreds of examples among the WPA's 250 thousand projects illustrate the boondoggling criticism. In Cleveland, $179 thousand was spent counting the same trees a private contractor was willing to count for $5 thousand. A rat extermination project in New Orleans ended costing $2.97 a rat. Twenty-one thousand dollars was spent placing two thousand street signs in Montgomery, Alabama, and $78,000 to repair a ditch in Denver, Colorado. After a 5 million-word history of New York City was written under the supervision of the WPA-sponsored Federal Arts Program, one critic pointed out that "the story of creation was written in 700 words, but not at government expense."[5]

Supporters of the WPA claimed that occasional cases of fraud or corruption were the fault of the local governments which, under the law, had to be the project's sponsors; and they said that the notion that private industry could do things cheaper was missing the point—private industry wasn't employing the unemployed. "If we can boondoggle ourselves out of this Depression," President Roosevelt exclaimed, "that word is going to be enshrined in the hearts of people for many years to come."[6]

Mr. Post Testifies

So widespread were charges of inefficiency in WPA projects that the House Appropriations Committee was directed to conduct an investigation. The following testimony is given by a consulting engineer, Chester Post, who investigated projects in Ohio for the U.S. Treasury. Some of the questions by Congressmen Johnson and Cannon indicate the conclusions that legislators are trying to draw from the testimony.

> *Mr. Ludlow:* I would like to get some light on the matter of labor efficiency. . . . On the building of highways, what proportion of labor is untrained and unskilled, just the common labor?

(Works Progress Administration)

WPA projects were undoubtedly less efficient than they could have been–but they gave work to an enormous number of men.

Mr. Post: Most of it is what would be classed as common labor. They may have a certain amount of experience in that particular kind of work.

Mr. Ludlow: . . .You say the labor on WPA projects is only 50 percent as efficient as labor on private projects. . . .is there something in the administrative regulations that makes for the inefficiency of labor on these projects? . . .

Mr. Post: A man taken from a factory, or from the white-collar class, may be perfectly physically sound, but he is what we would call soft and is not able to do a full day's work. . . .when you add that there is a certain amount of them who may not be willing to do a day's work, those factors tend to pull down efficiency.

Mr. Ludlow: I wondered whether there was anything inherent in the WPA system that would cause inefficiency in labor on these projects . . .

Mr. Post: . . . Private industry, PWA projects, and other governmental projects done by contract work do pick out the best, and what is left must be taken care of by WPA, as far as they will accept them at all as useful.

Mr. Ludlow: There are just as good people in the world in distress as those in industry, who have to work on WPA and if they work on WPA, I wondered how it is they are only 50 percent efficient, when in private construction the same people would be 100 percent efficient . . .

Mr. Roberts: Is it not true that you found with reference to those projects that large numbers of men were assigned to the projects without regard to the requirements of the project from the work supply standpoint?

Mr. Post: That is where the overmanning [too many men on one job] comes in.

Mr. Ludlow: In other words, there are men assigned to those projects, for instance, who ought not to be assigned to that kind of work; is that it?

Mr. Post: That does apply to overmanning.

Mr. Ludlow: They are misfits in this kind of work?

Mr. Post: Yes.

Mr. Cannon: Is it not true that the families of those men are just as much in need of food, shelter, and clothing as the families of the more efficient men?

Mr. Post: That is getting into an angle we did not go into.

Mr. Ditter: Are you qualifying as an engineer or as an economist?

Mr. Post: As an engineer.

Mr. Cannon: Whether an economist or an engineer, you know that every family has to have food, shelter, and clothing. Is not that the primary purpose of WPA? to provide food, shelter, and clothing for the families of unemployed workers?

Mr. Post: I think that is a matter for you to settle, and not for an engineer.

Mr. Cannon: It is a matter of such common knowledge as not to require demonstration [proof].

Mr. O'Neal: Is it not also a matter of common knowledge that with reasonable economy we can take care of many more workers if we can practice reasonable economy?

Mr. Post: That is true.

Mr. Roberts: How many projects altogether in Ohio did you inspect?

Mr. Post: Thirteen.

Mr. Johnson of West Virginia: If these thirteen projects you had inspected had been let to private industry on private contracts instead of the WPA undertaking to build these buildings, what would have been the saving on each of the thirteen?

Mr. Post: On those that we were able to analyze the cost in general ran twice or more than what we would estimate by private contract.

Mr. Cannon: But in doing that you gave men jobs who otherwise would not have had jobs, is not that true?

Mr. Post: You are getting into the economic basis of that.

Mr. Cannon: As a matter of fact, you know that is true, that men got jobs that would not have gotten jobs and their families were taken care of that would not have been taken care of. That is a matter of common knowledge.

Mr. Taber: We do not know whether that is true or not.

Mr. Cannon: I am surprised to hear the gentlemen from New York say that.

Mr. Taber: We know it is not a fact, because there would be a lot more people employed if it had not been for a lot of the crazy stuff that has been going on.

Mr. Cannon: The gentleman knows that thousands of men and their families have been taken care of who would not otherwise have been taken care of.

Mr. Johnson of West Virginia: Let me, in answer to Mr. Cannon's question, suggest this: Would it not have been about as cheap for the WPA to have taken these relief workers and paid them the difference between what it is costing the WPA to do the work as compared with the cost under private contract, and let them do nothing?

Mr. Post: I think so. Take a job where the efficiency is 33 1/3 percent, they would have employed too much labor. Your idea is to use the other amount and pay a dole [relief payment] to the men without work.

Mr. Johnson of West Virginia: Would it not be about as cheap for the Government, where there was that sort of a situation?

Mr. Post: I think in some cases that would have been true, but I would hate to generalize over the whole program.

Mr. Cannon: There is a difference between the dole [relief payment] and work. In your opinion, speaking just as a private citizen, do you think it is best to make paupers out of the people and give them the dole, or better to give them an opportunity to work?

Mr. Post: Our investigation was not such as to justify us in forming an opinion on that, Mr. Cannon.[7]

Re-establish WPA?

Charges of inefficiency and politics bedeviled the WPA during its entire eight-year history, as critics of WPA unceasingly demanded its elimination. Congress continued appropriating money for WPA projects, though never enough to employ all eligible workers, until World War II put an end to the need for relief. "No one," said Al Smith, "is going to shoot Santa Claus just before a hard Christmas." In the light of WPA's turbulent history, one must ask whether its faults were outweighed by its accomplishments; in the light of today's needs, one may also ask whether WPA projects should be established to aid Negroes and whites living in city slums where the unemployment rate is over 10 percent.

NOTES

1. Sherwin Smith, "Boondoggle that Helped 38 Million People," *New York Times Magazine,* May 2, 1965, p. 37.

2. Arthur M. Schlesinger, Jr., *The Politics of Upheaval* (Boston: Houghton Mifflin Company, 1960), pp. 345–346.

3. *Ibid.,* p. 246.

4. Donald S. Howard, *The WPA and Federal Relief Policy* (New York: Russell Sage Foundation, 1943), p. 126.

5. Sherwin Smith, *op. cit.,* pp. 72, 74.

6. *Ibid.,* p. 72.

7. United States Congress, House of Representatives, Committee on Appropriations, *Investigation and Study of the Works Progress Administration,* hearings before subcommittee, 76th Congress, 1st Session, on Resolution 130, April 11, 1939–June 13, 1939 (Washington, D.C.: U.S. Government Printing Office, 1939), pp. 712–713, 714–716.

QUESTIONS

1. Explain and analyze the logic behind the method of initiating and financing WPA projects.

2. Would the problem of providing work relief be solved by turning projects over to private industry?

3. Should the federal government today develop projects similar to WPA to aid Negroes and white who are living in city slums where the unemployment rate is over 10 percent.

SUGGESTED READING

Documents pertaining to the WPA which allow students to reach their own conclusions are collected by David Potter and William Goetzmann in *The New Deal and Employment* (New York: Holt, Rinehart & Winston, 1961). An excellent popular account of the WPA is the article by Sherwin D. Smith, "Boondoggle that Helped 38 Million People," *New York Times Magazine,* May 2, 1965. The standard scholarly work on the WPA is Donald S. Howard, *The WPA and Federal Relief Policy* (New York: Russell Sage Foundation, 1943). The best biographical account of relief for the unemployed is R. E. Sherwood, *Roosevelt and Hopkins* (New York: Harper & Row, Publishers, Inc., 1948).

Chapter 10
Keynes and the Multiplier

Introduction

It has been understood that the Depression was caused by the failure of total purchasing power to keep pace with production. During the 1920's economists generally assumed that savings were always funneled back into the flow of goods and services in the form of investments and that production therefore always created its own demand. President Herbert Hoover believed he could end the Depression simply by balancing the budget, restoring business confidence, and exhorting industry to produce. He believed the American economy was basically sound and required no corrective surgery by federal doctors. Like most leaders of his era, Hoover was schooled in the laissez-faire economics of Jean Say and Adam Smith. The economy, he believed, was essentially self-regulating and the un-fettered operation of the free market would bring recovery.

Four years of Hoover's policies failed to end the Depression. Unemployment mounted from 3.2 percent in 1929 to almost 25 percent in 1933; production declined by almost 50 percent. Since the economy did not respond to orthodox remedies, the assumptions of the classical economists were called into question. In 1936 John Keynes published *The General Theory of Employment, Interest, and Money,* which created a new school of economic thought and argued for government intervention in the economy. In brief, Keynes advised governments deliberately to create deficits and spend their way to recovery while orthodox economists advised balancing budgets and cutting federal expenditures.

Americans today are still divided over appropriate fiscal responses to depressions and recessions. They could fruitfully explore the aspects of Keynes' theory presented in this chapter to understand its departure from the old school of economics and the relationship of government expenditures to unemployment.

Gross National Product = Consumption + Investment + Government Spendings

It is essential to study some basic economic terms to clarify the ideas developed in this chapter. Economists measure a change in the country's economic health by comparing the Gross National Product (GNP) during several consecutive years. The Gross National Product is simply a measure in dollar values of all the products produced in the country during a given period of time, usually a year. The GNP may be subdivided into three basic parts.

1. *Consumption* expenditures *(C)*, which are by far the largest section of the GNP. These consist of the moneys spent by consumers within the following categories:

a) durables:* cars, furniture, washing machines and radios, etc.

b) semidurables: clothes, etc.

c) nondurables: food, beverages, etc.

d) services: doctors, private tutors, baby sitters, movies, etc.

2. *Investment* expenditures *(I)*, which are goods and services bought by businesses in order to produce more products. Business investment may be divided into the following categories:

a) plant and equipment: railroads, new factories, machinery, etc.

b) inventories: goods on the assembly line in the process of being made, or goods stored in warehouses and on store shelves.

In addition to business expenditures, investment includes residential construction, that is, the building of homes.

3. *Government* expenditures *(G)*, which include the moneys spent by government (state, federal, and local) on education, roads, unemployment relief, postal services, national defense, and other public services.

To summarize, Gross National Product = Consumption + Investment + Government expenditures, or $GNP = C + I + G$. In 1929, our GNP was $104.4 billion; in 1930 it was $91.1 billion; in 1932 it was $58.5 billion; these figures can be broken down as follows:

	Billion $		1929	1930	1932
Consumption	C	=	79.0	71.0	49.3
Investment	I	=	16.2	10.3	0.9
Government	G	=	8.5	9.2	8.1
Gross National Product	GNP**	=	104.4	91.2	58.5

The Multiplier

An analysis of the figures above reveals that the largest percent change between 1929, the last year of prosperity, and 1930, the first year of the Depression, was in investments. In fact, investments declined by 35 per-

---

*Note: a car purchased by a taxicab company and a washing machine purchased by a laundromat are classified as investment expenditures.

**The discrepancies in the total are due to net foreign investment, not included.

(The New York Times)

Uncle: But doctor, isn't it time she went on a diet?

1938, just before the "doctor" tried this course of treatment–with catastrophic results.

cent, while consumption only declined 10 percent.* By 1932, investments had decreased to $0.9 billion or by 95 percent, while consumption had decreased to $49.2 billion or 38 percent. Economists who have made intensive studies of the business cycle have discovered that this phenomenon usually accompanies economic fluctuations. Investment decreases much

---

*Changes in investment, 1929–30, created far greater changes in GNP; a $5.9 billion decrease in investment led to a $13.2 billion decrease in GNP.

more rapidly than consumption. Economists have generally concluded that depressions are caused by declines in business investment.*

Careful studies have been made of the relationship between GNP and investment. Economists have reached at least a tentative conclusion on this subject. Assuming that no other factors change, each dollar invested will increase GNP by three dollars. Likewise every dollar withheld from investment will reduce GNP by three dollars. Since each investment dollar will multiply through the economy approximately three times, this phenomenon is called the multiplier. Here is how it works.

Suppose Henry Ford decided to spend $100,000 in expansion of his Detroit factory. The money would either be paid directly to his workers, or to other businessmen who use it indirectly to pay their labor costs, or to pay dividends, etc. Studies have shown that workers and stockholders, on the average, spend about two-thirds of their incomes. Therefore, the recipients of Ford's $100,000 will probably save $33,000 and spend $67,000. The money spent will buy more food, clothes, cars, etc., thereby placing cash in the hands of grocers, haberdashers, and car salesmen. These individuals will spend two-thirds of that money on paying bills, and the money will go to more workers or stockholders, and so forth, in an endless chain until the entire $100,000 is exhausted. But look what this money has done to increase GNP:

stage 1. Ford's investment	$100,000
stage 2. Money spent by Ford's workers, 2/3 × $100,000 =	67,000
stage 3. Money spent by grocers, etc., 2/3 × $67,000 =	44,000
stage 4. Money spent by those receiving from above, 2/3 × $44,666 =	29,732
stage 5. Same as stage 4, except 2/3 × $29,732 =	19,821
stage 6. Same as stage 4, except 2/3 × $19,821 =	13,214
total to date =	274,433
stages 7–20 =	25,000
stage 21–infinity theoretical total =	300,000

Savings and Investments

The importance of business investment to the nation's economy should now be understood. Each additional dollar invested should result in a threefold increase in GNP.

Corporations invest savings of individuals or other businesses. They obtain these moneys by borrowing from banks, insurance companies, and by issuing stocks or bonds. Without access to these savings they could not find the funds to make more investments. Should these funds not be available, business investment falls off, causing a multiple contraction of GNP.

---

*This conclusion does not necessarily contradict early suppositions that depression was caused by a failure of purchasing power to keep pace with production, for it is precisely this failure that may have led worried businessmen to reduce their investments. In other words, when purchasing power no longer warranted a continued expansion, businessmen may have decided to cut back their investment expenditure. This conclusion is partially borne out by the fact that over 50 percent of the decline in investment came in two items, residential construction and business inventories.

Say's Law

The health of an economy depends on savings being channeled into investments. Though recognized today as a crucial problem, for many years economists assumed savings were always reinvested. This assumption was enshrined in a great unchallenged principle called Say's law. Other orthodox economists buttressed Say's beliefs with related assumptions. Temporary recessions would make investments less attractive, but would reduce interest rates. Therefore, money would again be funneled into productive enterprise. Similarly, unemployment would cause wages to decline, and thus increase the likelihood that workers would find gainful employment. In other words, the economy was assumed to be self-correcting. Wages, interest, savings, and investments all adjusted automatically in the free market when unencumbered by government controls. Any artificial interference with these free market forces would upset the natural balance. These faiths from the late nineteenth and early twentieth century formed the pool of economic wisdom which guided Herbert Hoover. They advised against deficit spending, government enterprise, or high taxes.

Keynes Advocates Deficit Spending

An Englishman, John Maynard Keynes, was much less optimistic about the automatic recovery powers of the economy. A writer and teacher by profession, he had made over $2 million in his spare time in the risky practice of buying and selling international currencies. During the 1930's, Keynes investigated Say's famous law and proclaimed it ridiculous. Savings are destroyed during depressions, Keynes observed, and therefore cannot be invested. Private enterprise is either unable or unwilling to invest. A nation may skid along at the bottom of a business cycle almost indefinitely; thus, contrary to Say there may be no automatic way out.

Having pronounced this gloomy prophecy, Keynes suggested a simple solution to depressions: when businessmen fail to sustain the economy with productive investment, government spending can be used to end the business downturn. The reasoning behind this revolutionary idea was disarmingly uncomplicated. Government spending would have the same multiplying effect as private investment; that is, the multiplier (see page 82) would be just as effective with government dollars as with private dollars. Therefore, according to Keynes, a nation could spend its way back to prosperity. The price for ending depressions is government budget deficits, caused by the emergency policy of heavy government spending.

A Summary

Both Say and Keynes would agree on the importance of savings and investments. However, Say assumed that investments and savings would always tend to equalize over the long run. In the long run, Keynes once said, we are all dead. The immediate problem was to restore the economy. Keynes advocated the revolutionary step of government expenditure to

Hope it holds out til the next grade.

Is this cartoonist a Keynesian?

supplement expenditure by private industry when insufficient to return all savings into the income flow. Keynes realized this course may unbalance the budget and he therefore advocated government deficits during depressions. The balance of this chapter is devoted to analyzing the relationship between investment, federal expenditure, and the economy.

Did Deficits Restore Prosperity?

Did Keynes' formula of federal spending work? President Hoover, as has been shown, tried to balance the budget, but failed. Franklin Roosevelt tried economizing in government, but he did not believe that a government could sit back and allow starvation. After Keynes came to the United States in 1934 and talked with the President, the economist confided to a friend that he had "supposed the president was more literate, economically speaking." Roosevelt was charmed by the Englishman: "I had a grand talk with K and like him immensely," but in 1936 Roosevelt informed an advisor that his greatest hope was to balance the budget.

Though President Roosevelt hoped to balance the budget, he never quite made it. Like Hoover, he thereby failed to spend as much as Keynes felt was needed to make deficit financing work. While Roosevelt's spending ran from $6 to $7 billion a year, with a deficit averaging $3 billion in 1934–35, Keynes felt that spending $12 to $15 billion a year was necessary for complete recovery. In 1936, Roosevelt announced he would try balancing his budget the following year and consequently reduced spending from $8.5 to $7.8 billion. The deficit, which was $3.5 billion in fiscal 1936, fell to $0.2 billion in 1937. Unemployment, which had fallen from approximately 13 million in 1933 to 7.7 million in 1937, rose again to 10.4 million in 1938. The rate of economic decline was even faster than between 1929 and 1933. Six or seven months after the onslaught of the "Roosevelt Recession," as the Republicans labeled this relapse, public work projects started again and unemployment declined to 9.5 million by 1939.

Noting the low deficits and high unemployment in America, Keynes concluded in 1940 that: "It is, it seems, politically impossible for a capitalistic democracy to organize expenditure in the scale necessary to make the grand experiment which would prove my case—except in war conditions."[1]

Arguments Against the Deficit

Other critics disapproved of the Keynes plan, not because of its politics, but because of its economics. The National Association of Manufacturers noted that deficit spending had not succeeded in providing *self-sustaining* economic growth, that is, although government spending temporarily benefited the economy, its failure was indicated by the collapse of the economy as soon as the federal stimulus was removed. The National Association of Manufacturers argued that:

> Deficit spending has actually discouraged a greater amount of new private spending that it has replaced. . . . It had little effect other than to cause . . . a staggering debt burden. Confronted by a government that is spending billions of dollars a year more than it takes in, the average investor is naturally cautious about making new long-range commitments. The investor notes that the debt incurred will have to be paid out of future earnings. He hesitates to embark on any new enterprise in the face of future drastic taxation. . . . The theory that by deficit financing we can achieve economic recovery overlooks the fact that government spending by itself cannot begin to provide the plant and equipment needed to put men back to work, that recovery is dependent on the stimulation of private investment, and that investors must be confident that private enterprise will be permitted to employ capital and labor properly.[2]

Debt or Unemployment

Do economic statistics support the argument of the National Association of Manufacturers? One should look at the record. It may be noted that private investment almost stopped completely by 1933, before Roosevelt began running annual deficits. So, considerations other than budget balancing influenced private enterprise's decisions on investing. The record shows that the federal government was unable to balance the budget or solve the unemployment problem throughout the 1930's and that business investment remained below the 1929 mark during the entire Depression. Finally, the record shows that during World War II the problem of unemployment was solved. By 1943, unemployment was completely eliminated, but government spending for the war had forced huge deficits, and the federal debt stood at $141 billion

GNP, EXPENDITURE, DEFICIT, AND UNEMPLOYMENT

Year	Total GNP	Total consumption expenditure	Total private investment	Federal, state, and local government expenditure	Federal surplus or deficit	Unemployment (percentage of total labor force)
	Billions of dollars					Percent
1929	104.4	79.0	16.2	8.5	+ 1.2	3.2
1930	91.1	71.0	10.3	9.2	+ .3	8.7
1931	76.3	61.3	5.5	9.2	− 2.1	15.9
1932	58.5	49.3	.9	8.1	− 1.5	23.6
1933	56.0	46.4	1.4	8.0	− 1.3	24.9
1934	65.0	51.9	2.9	9.8	− 2.9	21.7
1935	72.5	56.3	6.3	10.0	− 2.6	20.1
1936	82.7	62.6	8.4	11.8	− 3.5	16.9
1937	90.8	67.3	11.7	11.7	− .2	14.3
1938	85.2	64.6	6.7	12.8	− 2.0	19.0
1939	91.1	67.6	9.3	13.3	− 2.2	17.2
1940	100.6	71.9	13.2	14.1	− 1.4	14.6
1941	125.8	81.9	18.1	24.8	− 5.1	9.9
1942	159.1	89.7	9.9	59.7	−33.2	4.7
1943	192.5	100.5	5.6	88.6	−46.7	1.9
1944	211.4	109.8	7.1	96.5	−54.6	1.2

Source: United States Congress, 1964 Supplement to Economic Indicators, *Historical and Descriptive Background,* 88th Congress, 2nd Session (Washington, D.C., 1964), pp. 7, 33, 129.

NOTES

1. John Maynard Keynes, "The United States and the Keynes Plan," *The New Republic,* LXXXXIII (July 29, 1940), p. 158.
2. *Fallacies About Our Free Enterprise System* (National Association of Manufacturers, 1941), p. 26.

QUESTIONS

1. Explain why the multiplier works.
2. What was the basic disagreement between Say and Keynes?
3. Did deficit spending actually produce self-sustaining economic growth?

SUGGESTED READING

K.D. Roose's careful analysis of the recession of 1938 leads him to conclude that a cut in government spending was partially responsible for the downturn in business and that the subsequent increase in spending encouraged recovery. See his *The Economics of Recession and Revival* (New Haven: Yale University Press, 1954). Dudley Dillard *Economics of John Maynard Keynes* (New York: Prentice-Hall, 1948) explains the economist's theories in terms laymen will understand. Henry Hazlitt is highly critical of Keynes in *The Failure of the New Economics* (Princeton: D. Van Nostrand, 1959).

UNIT III.
THE WELFARE STATE

During the 1920's, conservatives like Andrew Mellon argued that individual initiative and private enterprise were the salvation of the poor, for wealth trickled down from the rich. Aid the poor, the theory went, and you destroy their initiative and make them ever dependent on government assistance. The widespread misery of the 1930's challenged these arguments, and President Roosevelt began using the federal government to help people living in depressed areas (like the Tennessee Valley), to provide security for people over 65, to help workers and farmers, and to provide protection for stock market investors. Finally, Roosevelt proposed taxing the rich in order to pay for these programs. For better or worse, Roosevelt started a trend toward a welfare state based on the assumption that the federal government has the responsibility to aid those citizens unable to provide for themselves. This unit presents the programs developed by Roosevelt and gives arguments for and against them. The reader must decide what responsibilities the American government has in aiding its citizens.

(Farm Security Agency)

Chapter 11
The Tennessee Valley Authority

Introduction

The Tennessee Valley yielded fortunes to cotton planters before the Civil War and to lumber barons years later. By 1920 the resources of the seven state area were exhausted and its 4.5 million inhabitants were proud but poor people. The Valley's major asset was a half-completed dam and nitrate plant at Muscle Shoals which the federal government had abandoned after the Armistice of 1918 ended the need for explosives. Henry Ford offered to buy the plant to manufacture cheap fertilizers and to use the extra electricity to develop the lower valley. Because Senator George Norris dreamed of coordinate development of the entire valley, Congress refused to sell Ford the facilities at Muscle Shoals. Norris' dream became a reality when President Franklin Roosevelt supported the establishment of the Tennessee Valley Authority to build sixteen dams along the Tennessee and its tributaries. These provided flood control, navigation, reforestation, and a host of other services in addition to cheap electricity. To many Americans, TVA stands as a monument to what may be achieved through federal coordination of an area's resources. But the debate over public and private development continues to this day, and the Tennessee Valley still looms as a controversial case of government intervention in economic affairs. This chapter allows the reader to examine the issue of regional planning and determine for himself whether public or private development of resources in an underdeveloped area is the more desirable.

Ford's Proposal

Henry Ford, whose Model T had given his country cheap motor transportation, stood before the half-finished government dam at Muscle Shoals on December 5, 1921. Before him stretched the mighty Tennessee River and his mind was filled with a vision of prosperity for the Valley. Next to Ford stood Thomas A. Edison, the great inventor, who had offered his services to help make the manufacturer's vision become a reality. What did Ford have in mind? What was he planning for the Tennessee?

Henry Ford had offered to buy the half-deserted nitrate plant built by the government at Muscle Shoals during World War I to make materials needed for explosives. Ford proposed to manufacture cheap fertilizer at this plant and sell it to farmers at half the usual price. He would limit his profits to 8 percent. The plant had cost the government $82 million, but many thought it a white elephant once the war ended, and Ford offered $5 million for it. In addition he would buy the Wilson dam at Muscle Shoals (once the government completed it) and pay 6 percent of the completion costs annually (for the electricity this plant would produce) and another 4 percent annually (as rent on a 100-year lease) to repay the government's construction costs. Ford proposed to use the electricity not needed to produce fertilizer in private enterprises he would sponsor, to manufacture aluminum, cloth, steel, automobile parts, and the like.

Six weeks after his visit to Muscle Shoals, Ford publicized his dream for the poverty-stricken Tennessee Valley. He would build a 75-mile city, a second Detroit, only larger. He would employ a million men; he would protect the health and welfare of his workers and their families. He would then turn this fabulous new city over to either federal or state governments so that neither he nor his heirs would make a personal profit.

Congress's Dilemma

Ford's offer raised troublesome questions, and Congress was not convinced it should accept. Were Ford's motives as pure as he claimed? How could Ford be sure that he could produce such cheap fertilizer? Was Ford's dream city a sincere public plan or a self-interested public relations gimmick? Should facilities built at such great public cost be turned over to one man in whose hands now would rest the fate of all the lower valley? Would the sale be an extravagant gift to one of the richest men in the United States? And finally, what about the private power companies already in the Valley? Could they compete against Henry Ford once the federal government gave him such special privileges?

These were not easy questions to answer and Congress took its time. Lengthy hearings began in both the House and the Senate (1922–1923) and an endless parade of witnesses was called to testify on Ford's proposal. The House committee finally reported the bill favorably and on March 10, 1924, the House voted 227–143 to accept Ford's offer. However, George Norris, head of the Senate committee, was determined to block Ford, who, he thought, wanted to get cheap electric power for his own industries at a fraction of its cost. He kept the bill bottled up while his committee listened to competing bills for private electric power to develop Muscle Shoals. But Norris' real hope was to have the federal government develop the Tennessee Valley. Eventually his agricultural committee reported out Norris' bill for a carefully planned development of the entire Tennessee River watershed under government direction.

Norris' report did not prevent the Senate from acting on Ford's bid.

But in October, 1924, Henry Ford withdrew his offer, expressing disgust with Congressional delay: "A single affair of business which should have been decided by anyone within a week has become a complicated political affair."[1]

Public or Private Power

Elated by his victory over Ford, George Norris defined the issue. "The struggle over Muscle Shoals simplified itself to an issue between those who believed in public ownership and development of the power at Muscle Shoals and throughout the entire Tennessee Valley, and the 'power trust' seeking to prevent everything of the kind."[2]

The victorious senator now threw himself into the fight for public power. Norris defeated Union Carbide's bid to purchase Muscle Shoals by demonstrating it meant $1.6 to $7.3 million yearly profit for the company. Finally, Norris was successful in passing his own recommendation through Congress for federal development of Muscle Shoals and other dams. But President Calvin Coolidge refused to sign this bill, killing it with a pocket veto. Several years later Norris' effort drew the full measure of Herbert Hoover's wrath. In a strongly worded veto message, Hoover implied the proposal was socialistic:

> I am firmly opposed to the government entering into any business, the major purpose of which is competition with our citizens. . . . For the federal government deliberately to go out to build up and expand an occasion to the major purpose of a power and manufacturing business is to break down the initiative and enterprise of the American people; it is destruction of equality of opportunity of our people; it is the negation of the ideas upon which our civilization has been based.
>
> . . . This bill would launch the federal government upon a policy of ownership and operation of power utilities upon a basis of competition. . . I hesitate to contemplate the future of our institutions, of our country if the preoccupation of its officials is to be no longer the promotion of justice and equal opportunity, but is to be devoted to barter in the markets. That is not liberalism, it is degeneration.[3]

The Tennessee Valley Authority Is Established

Imagine ex-President Hoover's indignation two years later when his successor, Roosevelt, urged Congress to go beyond Norris' original suggestions and develop the entire Tennessee Valley. Roosevelt envisioned government protection and development of all the resources of the valley:

> It is clear that the Muscle Shoals development is but a small part of the potential public usefulness of the entire Tennessee River. Such use, if envisioned in its entirety, transcends mere power development; it enters the wide fields of flood control, soil erosion, afforestation, elimination from agricultural use of marginal lands, and distribution and diversification of industry. In short, this power development of war days leads logically to national planning for a complete river watershed involving many states and the future lives and welfare of millions. It touches and gives life to all forms of human concerns.

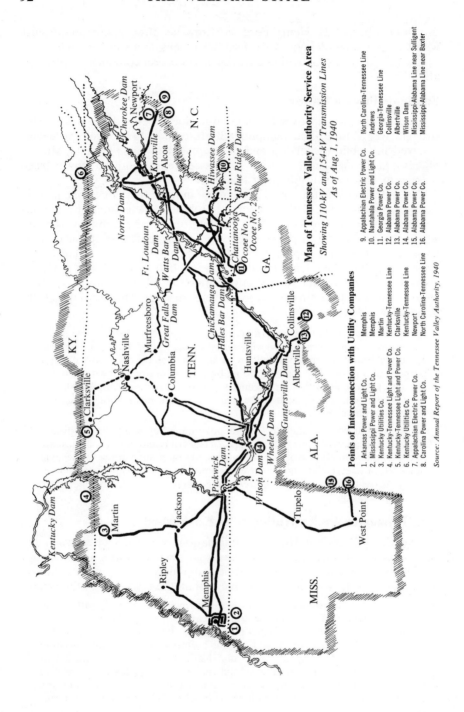

Map of Tennessee Valley Authority Service Area

*Showing 110-kV and 154-kV Transmission Lines
As of Aug. 1, 1940*

Points of Interconnection with Utility Companies

1. Arkansas Power and Light Co.	Memphis	
2. Mississippi Power and Light Co.	Memphis	
3. Kentucky Utilities Co.	Martin	
4. Kentucky-Tennessee Light and Power Co.	Clarksville	Kentucky-Tennessee Line
5. Kentucky-Tennessee Light and Power Co.	Clarksville	Kentucky-Tennessee Line
6. Kentucky Utilities Co.	Newport	Kentucky-Tennessee Line
7. Appalachian Electric Power Co.		North Carolina-Tennessee Line
8. Carolina Power and Light Co.		North Carolina-Tennessee Line
9. Appalachian Electric Power Co.		Andrews
10. Nantahala Power and Light Co.		Georgia-Tennessee Line
11. Georgia Power Co.		Collinsville
12. Alabama Power Co.		Albertville
13. Alabama Power Co.		Wilson Dam
14. Alabama Power Co.		Mississippi-Alabama Line near Sulligent
15. Alabama Power Co.		Mississippi-Alabama Line near Baxter
16. Alabama Power Co.		

Source: Annual Report of the Tennessee Valley Authority, 1940.

I, therefore, suggest to the Congress legislation to create a Tennessee Valley Authority, a corporation clothed with the power of government but possessed of the flexibility and initiative of a private enterprise. It should be charged with the broadest duty of planning for the proper use, conservation and development of the natural resources of the Tennessee River drainage basin and its adjoining territory for the general social and economic welfare of the nation. This Authority should also be clothed with the necessary power to carry these plans into effect. . . .[4]

Within weeks the dynamic Congress of the 100 days translated Roosevelt's proposal into law. On June 8, 1933, Roosevelt ordered construction to begin; less than three years later the Norris dam was completed and in operation. Within ten years, fifteen more dams were completed. One, the Fontana Dam, was as high as a forty-six story building, while a second, the Cherokee Dam, was built in sixteen months, a world's record until its twin, the Douglas, was built in twelve months. Construction, in the words of one laborer, was "one hell of a big job of work." The sixteen dams held enough concrete to fill the seven great pyramids of Egypt twelve times over, 113 million cubic yards. A navigable channel was dug 9 feet deep and 650 miles long. The "great lakes" that rose behind these dams were three-quarters the size of Rhode Island. By 1939, TVA was supplying cheap electrical power to 180 thousand customers; the same year TVA bought out the Tennessee Electric Power Company, after a long and bitter fight in the courts, and added another 150 thousand customers to its rolls. By 1964, TVA was selling and transmitting over $160 million worth of electric power each year, enough to serve almost 2 million families.*

Opposition to TVA

Naturally, this multimillion-dollar public enterprise aroused unrelenting opposition from men and women who, like President Hoover, felt the federal government should not produce power in competition with private industry. Leaders of the battle waged against the TVA were the private power companies that had been selling to customers in the Tennessee Valley. Government power production killed their potential market and forced some, like the Tennessee Power Company, to sell out. Opposition to TVA also came from citizens who feared national planning and government ownership as the road to socialism. If the government could run electric power companies out of business, what industry was next—steel, automobile, medicine, railroads? Would government control stop short of complete domination?

TVA and the Danger to Freedom

The danger, thought apostles of laissez-faire, was not to private enterprise alone. Government control could mean the end of everybody's freedom. As even the one-time director of TVA, David Lilienthal, admitted:

---

*In 1964, 77 percent of TVA power was generated by steam rather than by water-turned generators.

TVA, *if* it were politically managed, could become a curse to this valley. Just what would it mean if politics had been injected into TVA's selection of personnel, or into detailed administration of funds by which the job is carried out? It would mean that thousands of miles of transmission lines built by TVA's forces might have been located not for economic and engineering reasons, but upon a political basis. A city that votes "right," a county that delivers the "right" number of votes for a particular organization or candidate, an industry that "comes through," could be rewarded by advantages in the location of transmission lines, though such a location was not justified by the business facts. A city and its industries that do not vote "right" might find that its electric sub-stations were not adequately maintained, that service was poor, that its industrial growth had stopped.[5]

And yet, a somewhat typical operation of TVA, with its emphasis on the development of the entire valley, including its human and physical resources, went something like the following. Under the original terms of the TVA Act the federal government was required to operate the fertilizer plant at Muscle Shoals. Rather than risk producing fertilizer not needed in the valley, TVA officials started consulting with local experts to find what types of fertilizers would be most beneficial. A small test plant was then built to start producing this fertilizer. Farmers were invited to participate in this experiment by getting free use of the fertilizer in exchange for keeping careful records of its effects on crops, so their neighbors would learn of the benefits. Farmers were also taught by agricultural experts that certain crops like corn and tobacco robbed the soil of vital minerals. Because they needed the money from cash crops to pay their bills, poor farmers could not afford to plant soil-replenishing grasses. TVA officials therefore experimented with low-cost refrigerator methods which would

(Tennessee Valley Authority)

Wilson Dam, TVA.

**Comparison of Average Annual Consumption
and Annual Cost of Domestic Service**

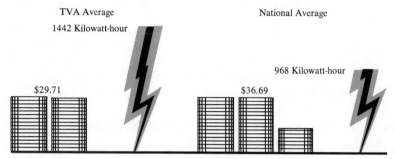

Source: *Annual Report of the Tennessee Valley Authority, 1941*

reduce the farmers' need for cash. Out of this program came a community freezer which enabled farmers to save money by storing meats. A quick-freezer unit for strawberries was also invented and sold to private industry for further development. Farmers in the valley now not only save money by using community freezers, but have developed a profitable strawberry industry, and the sale of the frozen berries supplies them with the cash needed to buy fertilizers and restore their lands. Meanwhile a hay drier was developed by TVA and sold to private industry for commercial production and farmers in the valley now make a profit from planting soil-conserving grasses.

The fertilizer story does not refute the charges of possible government suppression and of competition with private enterprise. It merely illustrates one of many activities in which TVA officials and farmers worked together to develop the Tennessee River Valley in the interest of all, private enterprise included. Other and more specific charges levied against TVA need further examination.

Accusation and Response: TVA and Flood Control

A businessman and economist, Dean Russell, in his book *The TVA Idea,* charges that by July, 1947, TVA had allocated $153 million in construction costs for flood control. The yearly interest cost to the taxpayer on this investment is at least $3.5 million. Yet TVA, by its own estimation, admitted that the average yearly flood damage on the Tennessee River was only $1.5 million before 1933.

Furthermore, to prevent $1.5 million yearly flood damage, Russell claims that TVA permanently flooded 463 thousand acres of land behind its twenty-one dams, and holds another 128 thousand acres in reserve. But the army engineers estimated that only once every 500 years would the Tennessee River temporarily flood as much territory as the TVA flooded permanently and holds in reserve. The value of crops lost in this flooding was estimated in 1941 at $13.4 million.

In its annual report of 1964 the TVA claimed:

Regulation of floods in March and April 1964 averted about $1 million in damage at Chattanooga, Tenn., bringing damages averted at that point to $252 million.

Damage of $3-1/4 million was averted along the Ohio-Mississippi by reduction of three flood crests during high water in the period March into May, 1964, bringing the total damage averted in this area to $39 million since 1945.

Total damages averted in the Tennessee and Ohio-Mississippi basins reached $316 million, almost twice the investment in TVA flood control facilities.[6]

Accusation and Response: Spending and Saving on Navigation

In his book *The TVA Idea,* Dean Russell charges that 193 million ton miles of freight were shipped on the Tennessee River in 1946 at a cost to the government of 4.13 cents a ton. In this same year, the average rate per ton mile on Southern railroads was 1 cent. In other words, it cost the taxpayer about $8 million to save shippers approximately $2 million.

According to the 1964 Annual Report of the Tennessee Valley Authority, in 1963:

Ton miles of traffic totaled 2.2 billion, a slight decline from 1962. The preliminary estimate of savings to shippers during the year was $21.4 million, exceeding Federal costs of operating and maintaining the channel by $15.9 million. Cumulative annual savings to shippers since 1933 reached $282 million. Cumulative annual costs for the same period were $91.5 million.[7]

TVA: An Unfair Competitor of Public Utilities

Dean Russell claimed that TVA could undersell private power companies, since it pays no federal taxes. Although it did pay 5.5 percent of its operating revenue of 1947 instead of state and local taxes, in 1947 private utility companies payed 18.9 percent of their revenues in state, local, and *federal* taxes.

According to the 1964 Annual report of the Tennessee Valley Authority:

A total of more than $22.8 million in tax equivalents and in lieu payments was made on TVA power in the 1964 fiscal year, an increase of $2.4 million over 1963. . . . The combined total . . . amounted to 7.5% of the combined electric operating revenues. . . . In comparison, state and local taxes (not federal) of 12 privately owned public utility (companies) adjacent to TVA ranged from 4.5% to 10.6% of their revenues.[8]

TVA and Cheap Electricity

In 1933, it was widely believed that private companies were charging outrageously high prices for electricity. One major argument for TVA at that time was that it would establish a yardstick by which government-generated electric rates could be compared to rates charged by private industry. TVA claimed that it was able to reduce electric rates and still operate profitably because rate reduction increased the use of electricity and

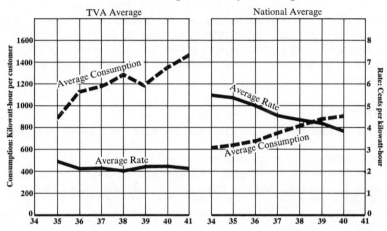

Residential Average Rate and Consumption
United States Average and TVA System Average

Source: Annual Report of the Tennessee Valley Authority, 1941

the costs of generating electricity were far lower than the costs of stringing transmission lines. TVA officials boasted they were so successful in their experiment that private power companies started imitating TVA and reducing rates to attract more customers. Dean Russell and the private utilities argued that TVA rates were lower only because TVA did not pay taxes or interest on loans and therefore really operated at a loss. Up to 1947, the cost of borrowing the money to build TVA by private enterprise would have been approximately $200 million in interest. It cost TVA absolutely nothing because the money was lent free of charge by the federal government and the taxpayer was billed for interest. Today TVA borrows money by issuing bonds which it must repay.

According to the 1964 Annual Report of TVA:

> Residential use of electricity increased to 10,818 kilowatt-hours per customer for the year at an average rate of 0.92 cents per kilowatt-hour, compared with national averages of 4,548 kilowatt-hours and 2.34 cents.
>
> Payments to the U.S. Treasury from power revenues were $50.2 million, bringing total payments to more than $447'million.[9]

More Projects Like TVA?

The TVA controversy is far from dead even today. In 1937, George Norris tried drumming up interest for another valley authority, this time on the Columbia River. Lyndon Johnson was among fourteen senators sponsoring a bill for a second TVA; Roosevelt had plans for seven other river projects. Senator Barry Goldwater, the Republican presidential candidate in 1964, has frequently advocated selling parts of TVA to private enterprise. In 1965, Secretary of Interior Stewart Udall accompanied local congressmen down the Connecticut River to determine what recommendations should be made to restore and save its natural beauty. Every year floods destroy several million dollars of property within the Mississippi watershed. Private electrical rates are still higher than those charged by TVA. Nevertheless, those opposed to extending federal power defeat proposals for additional federal river projects and their arguments are frequently based on the TVA experience.

NOTES

1. Preston Hubbard, *Origins of the TVA* (Nashville: Vanderbilt University Press, 1961), p. 138.

2. *Ibid.,* p. 147.

3. *Congressional Record,* 71st Congress, 3rd Session, pp. 7046–7048.

4. Franklin D. Roosevelt, *The Public Papers and Addresses of Franklin D. Roosevelt,* ed. Samuel I. Rosenman, vol. II (New York: Random House, 1938), p. 122.

5. David Lilienthal, *TVA—Democracy on the March* (New York: Harper & Row, Publishers, Inc., 1944).

6. Tennessee Valley Authority, *Annual Report of the Tennessee Valley Authority, 1964,* (Washington, D.C.: U.S. Government Printing Office, 1964), p. 5.

7. *Ibid.,* p. 3.

8. *Ibid.,* pp. 41–42.

9. *Ibid.,* p. 5.

QUESTIONS

1. Do the advantages outweigh the dangers when the federal government rather than private industry develops a region? Explain.

2. After considering Hoover's warnings, Russell's charges, and TVA's record, do you judge TVA a success? Explain.

3. In the light of the experience under TVA, would you support similar projects in other regions?

SUGGESTED READING

P. J. Hubbard tells the story of Ford's offer and its ultimate rejection in *Origins of the TVA* (Nashville: Vanderbilt University Press, 1961). David E. Lilienthal, *TVA: Democracy on the March* (New York: Harper & Row, Publisher, Inc., 1944) is the standard account, and Philip Selzneck, *The TVA and the Grass Roots, A Study in the Sociology of Formal Organization* (Berkeley: University of California Press, 1949), one of the more scholarly works in the field, deals primarily with the issue of decentralization. For a critique of TVA see Dean Russell, *The TVA Idea* (Irvington-on-Hudson, N.Y.: Foundation for Economic Education, 1949). On George Norris see Alfred Lief, *Democracy's Norris* (New York: Stackpole Sons, 1939).

Chapter 12

The Farmer and the Agricultural Adjustment Act

Introduction

The Great Depression of the 1930's was preceded and, to some extent, caused by the farm depression of the 1920's. The attempt to aid farmers with the McNary-Haugen Act failed, since conservative presidents vetoed the plan. But, in 1929, a federal Farm Board was established and given $500 million to purchase and store farm surpluses. However, the Board was powerless to maintain farm prices in the face of the worldwide depression that began that year. As farm commodities sank to prices as low as those prevailing in Elizabethan England, and as large numbers of families were bankrupt and forced off their lands, farmers began taking the law into their own hands. Some farmers forcibly prevented the marketing of crops in the hopes of driving prices up. Others interrupted sheriffs' sales of bankrupt farms by threatening judges with reprisals.

The Agricultural Adjustment Act of 1933 introduced a radical new principle into farm policy. For the first time in history the government actually paid farmers not to plant their crops and it even paid them to destroy crops already planted. In addition, the government pledged to buy up agricultural surpluses and hold them off the market to raise prices. These programs achieved their object of raising farm income, but also increased food costs and scarcities while millions the world over went to bed hungry every night. And though this program was considered a temporary expedient to tide America over a crisis, crop restriction is still the federal farm policy.

Bunker Hill 20

The outpost on highway 20 leading into Sioux City, Iowa, was known as Bunker Hill 20. A dozen or more farmers were camped by the roadside, armed with bricks, axe handles, and spiked planks. Their mission was to prevent trucks with farm produce from entering the town. Other farmers blockaded more highways leading into Sioux City. And throughout the states of Iowa, Nebraska, and North and South Dakota desperate debt-ridden farmers were taking similar action: stopping trucks, dumping milk over roads, defying armed deputies, and removing badges from sheriffs. Iowa's governor, Dan Turner, sat helplessly in the state capital. He dared not call out troopers to clear the roads for he had to run for re-election.

Talk at the Barricades

They say blockading the highway's illegal. I says, Seems to me there was a Tea-party in Boston that was illegal too. What about destroying property in Boston Harbor when our country was started?

When we can't buy there can't be any prosperity. We ain't been buying nothing, not for four years.[1]

So spoke the farmers manning the outpost called Bunker Hill 20. They thought their revolution was as necessary to save their homes from foreclosure as the American Revolution was to save other Americans from British tyranny. Per capita farm income was down to $48 a year, and it seemed that something had to be done.

The Agricultural Adjustment Act

Eight months after farmers at Bunker Hill 20 voluntarily called off their strike and returned to their farms, Congress passed a measure designed to help dissatisfied farmers all over the country. Even though the bill did not satisfy farm strike leader Milo Reno, or his more radical following, it did signal a far-reaching departure from previous farm policy.

President Roosevelt signed the Agricultural Adjustment Act into law on May 12, 1933. It promised relief through benefit payments to farmers who agreed to reduce their acreage in one of the seven basic farm commodities: wheat, cotton, field corn, hogs, rice, tobacco, or dairy products. (The list was later extended to fifteen.) Payments would be financed by a processing tax paid by millers, bakers, textile manufacturers, etc.*

The purpose of AAA was fourfold: (1) to grant immediate relief to the farmer through benefit payments; (2) to increase prices for farm products by crop reduction; (3) to provide for government purchase at higher prices and government storing; and (4) to help consumers as well as farmers by providing surpluses for lean years when crops failed.

Evolution and Operation of Crop Reduction

Thoughtful farm leaders had long realized one basic cause of the farm problem was simply too much produce. But how to reduce the surplus? During the 1920's, George Peek and Hugh Johnson advocated that government buy the domestic surplus and sell it abroad. But the McNary-Haugen Bill was vetoed twice by President Coolidge. His successor, Herbert Hoover, had reluctantly permitted the federal government to start buying and storing farm surpluses and, as a result, the government bought several million tons of grain but could not maintain farm prices. Farm leaders fi-

---

*Later revisions of AAA substituted payments to farmers from general taxation instead of payments from taxes on the processers.

nally decided surpluses could only be reduced by reducing acreage. The farmer, however, could not be persuaded to cut back his crops unless given assurance that his neighbor would do the same thing and that cheaters would not benefit from the sacrifices made by their friends.

The Agricultural Adjustment Act ingeniously devised a technique for securing farmers' voluntary cooperation to save agriculture and themselves. Each farmer would agree to reduce his own crop by a specified percent, always less than 20, and sign a contract with the federal government. Sometime before the harvest, a county agent selected by local farmers visited each farm in the county to check whether the contract terms were followed. The farmer who lived up to his contract would receive an amount of money approximately equal to the yield of the acres he did not sow in the restricted crop. The farmer, however, was encouraged to plant soil-replenishing grasses on this vacated ground. If he broke his agreement with the government or if he simply refused to sign a contract, he would not be eligible for benefit payments or other forms of federal assistance. No major crop would be reduced under AAA unless two-thirds of the farmers producing that commodity first agreed to production controls through a referendum.

Parity

It was hoped that aid to the farmer would eventually restore agricultural prices to the buying power farmers enjoyed from 1910 to 1914. In other words, if a bushel of wheat would buy a pair of dungarees in 1914, it should also buy one in 1933. This ratio between the prices farmers were charged and the prices they received is known as *parity*, and government still tries to support farm prices at some fixed percent of parity.

The Agricultural Adjustment Act of 1933 and subsequent farm bills have sought to help farmers achieve parity. One way of achieving parity was by controlling production. In addition the AAA was given power to buy and store crops and gradually dispose of surpluses.

Plowing Cotton Under and Killing Little Pigs

While Congress was debating the Agricultural Adjustment Act, farmers were already plowing and planting. When Roosevelt signed the Act, the 1933 crop was already sprouting. The cotton harvest in particular promised to be a good one—17 million bales of cotton were predicted. But this abundance meant ruin to its producers. Thirteen million bales of cotton were left unsold from the previous harvest, and prices were threatening to fall to 5 cents a pound, which was less than the cost of raising the cotton. Henry Wallace, Secretary of Agriculture, swung into action. Contracts were signed with 1 million farmers and $100 million dollars were paid to them in benefits. Farmers were paid to plow under one-fourth of their cotton acreage—a total of 10 million acres.

With corn selling at only 35 cents a bushel, farmers were feeding it to their hogs. But with hog prices down to 2.5 cents a pound, hog producers could not earn a living. They asked the government to buy and slaughter

(Standard Oil of New Jersey)

Cotton pickers' cabins in Mississippi; what happened to these families when the plantation owner plowed his cotton under, or bought a mechanical picker?

6 million little pigs. Approximately 100 million pounds were saved and distributed to the unemployed; the remainder was made into grease or fertilizer. Many shared the resentment expressed in a voter's letter to Wallace: "It just makes me sick all over when I think how the government has killed millions and millions of little pigs, and how that has raised pork prices until we poor people can not even look at a piece of bacon."[2]

Henry Wallace was not happy about slaughtering pigs and burying cotton. The descendent of a long line of agricultural statesmen, Wallace wanted people fed, not food destroyed. "Only the merest quarter-turn of the heart," he informed an Iowa audience in 1933, "separates us from a material abundance beyond the fondest dreams of anyone present."[3] But Wallace also criticized "those standpat sentimentalists who weep that farmers should practice controlled production [and] do not suggest that clothing factories go on producing ad infinitum, regardless of effective demand for their merchandise, until every naked Chinaman is clad."[4] And the Secretary was the more indignant because industry cut back its production by over $20 billion between 1929 and 1933. Was this not far more damnable than plowing under a few surplus crops to save farmers from bankruptcy and ruin?

> The pig-iron reduction control of the big steel companies in 1933 was in principle one-thousand times as damnable as the pig reduction campaign of 1933. Pig iron [used in making steel] in 1932 was about 20 percent of that in 1929. Pig production in 1933 in pounds was 97 percent of that in 1929. . . .

In other words, farmers cut pig production 3 percent when steel companies cut pig-iron production 80 percent. That sort of industrial production program plowed millions of workers out into the streets. It is because of that industrial reduction program that we have to spend billions for relief to keep the plowed-out workers from starvation. I hope industry in future reduction programs will not find it desirable to plow millions of workers out of their jobs. People are more important than pigs.[5]

Wallace defended the "plow up" and the "pig kill" as only means of operating in a society based on the profit motive. Norman Thomas, a socialist, criticized the AAA program as symbolic of a society which "crowded families together in shacks and slums and hovels while the builders of skyscrapers are idle." Only in America were the "bread lines knee deep in wheat."[6] The Agricultural Adjustment Act, Thomas claimed, was an indictment of American society, for it admitted that

There was no way to restore a partial prosperity to farmers except to produce an artificial scarcity by paying agricultural producers from proceeds of a tax on consumers to destroy the abundance of foodstuffs which man struggled thousands upon thousands of years to be able to create. And this, be it remembered, in the midst of a cold and hungry world. The more sincerely one believes that such legislation was an emergency necessity the more terrible is the indictment of the civilization which brought it about.[7]*

Wheat and Drought

While Henry Wallace wrestled with problems imposed by corn, hog, and cotton surpluses, he also faced the problem of wheat for which there was no market. With abundant acres of winter wheat long in the ground, it seemed that Wallace would have to order another plow-up. But nature came to the rescue of the Department of Agriculture and saved it from the embarrassment of plowing under wheat while in every major city hungry people waited in bread lines. Years of careless farming, bad weather, and severe droughts created dust storms that blew Kansas topsoil 200 miles over the Atlantic and devastated wheat crops in a destructive act of nature more drastic than any reduction ever contemplated by the AAA. The wheat harvest was cut by one-third; prices shot skyward. In 1935 and 1936, faced with shortage, Americans actually imported wheat.

Agriculture to 1941

After 1933, the Department of Agriculture had more time to devise production controls, and crop reduction was carried out by methods far less drastic than plowing them into the ground. Farmers planned their own acreage restrictions with county agents, following the guidelines of national policy and needs. In return, the government disbursed benefit pay-

---

*The federal farm program was not limited to paying farmers cash for reducing their harvest. Between 1933 and 1940 the federal government spent over $0.5 billion distributing surplus foods to needy individuals on relief. By 1940 the government was experimenting with a food stamp program under which low-income families could purchase surplus foods in their grocery stores. In recent years, similar programs have been reactivated with considerable success.

ments; farm income edged up 50 percent by 1941. The processing tax was killed by a Supreme Court decision in 1936, but Congress in 1936 and 1938 re-enacted farm legislation to make crop reduction more acceptable to the Court. To meet Supreme Court objections, farmers were to be paid from the general tax funds instead of processing taxes, and crop restrictions were tied to soil conservation measures. But the program was effectively the same.

By 1941, it was possible to sit back and take stock of the entire program. Study these figures carefully to decide whether the farm program was a success.[8]

Year	Farm income without federal aid	Gov. payments to farmers	Farm income including payments
1918–20 (Avg.)	$11,290 mil.	$000 mil.	$11,290 mil.
1929	11,304	000	11,304
1930	9,048	000	9.048
1931	6,372	000	6,372
1932	4,640	000	4,640
1933	5,160	276	5,436
1934	6,119	637	6,756
1935	7,137	507	7,644
1936	8,225	415	8,640
1937	8,696	460	9,156
1938	7,652	496	8,148
1939	7,812	768	8,580
1940	8,347	713	9.060
1941	10,963	653	11,616

Notice that farm income increased far more rapidly than the actual amount of direct government payments to farmers. Notice also that by 1941 farm income exceeded pre-Depression levels and note the dip in farm income during the recession year of 1938. What factor probably accounts for the relatively rapid increase in farm income between 1939 and 1941, despite the reduced benefit payments? Why would farm income increase faster than federal farm expenditures? Who pays the bill for the farm program?

The chart below shows you the effects of the farm program on both acreage and production. Note that acreage reduction often failed to cause crop reduction; yields per acre increased rapidly because of more efficient farming.[9]

Crop	Acreage before AAA 1931–33 avg.	Production before AAA 1931–33 avg.	Acreage under AAA 1940–42 avg.	Production under AAA 1940–42 avg.	Percent change acres	prod.
Corn	110.0 mil.	2635 mil. bu.	89.0 mil.	2757 mil. bu.	−20	+ 5
Wheat	67.2	750 mil. bu.	58.7	910 mil. bu.	−13	+21
Cotton	38.6	14.4 mil. bale	23.8	12 mil. bale	−38	−17
Tobacco	1.7	1318 mil. lb.	1.4	1377 mil. lbs.	−18	+ 4

The following chart shows the effects on wheat and cotton prices and also on the parity ratio of prices received by all farmers and prices paid by all farmers.

	Wheat price per bushel (dollars)	Cotton price per 100 lbs (dollars)	Farm parity ratio
1932	.38	6.52	55
1933	.74	10.17	60
1934	.85	12.36	70
1935	.83	11.09	84
1936	1.03	12.36	90
1937	.96	8.41	92
1938	.56	8.60	77
1939	.69	9.09	77
1940	.68	9.89	80
1941	.95	17.03	94
1942	1.10	19.04	106
1943	1.36	19.88	119
1944	1.41	20.73	116

Source: United States Bureau of the Census, *Historical Statistics of the United States, 1789–1945* (Washington, D.C., 1949), pp. 99, 106, 108.

NOTES

1. Mary Heaton Vorse, "Rebellion in the Cornbelt," *Harpers,* CLXVI (December, 1932), p. 5.

2. Henry A. Wallace, *Democracy Reborn* (New York: Harcourt Brace & World, Inc., 1944), p. 103.

3. Arthur M. Schlesinger, Jr., *The Coming of the New Deal* (Boston: Houghton Mifflin Company, 1958), p. 64.

4. *Ibid.,* p. 63.

5. Wallace, *op. cit.,* p. 105.

6. Norman Thomas, *The Choice Before Us* (New York: The Macmillan Company, 1934), p. 6.

7. *Ibid.,* p. 7.

8. United States Congress, Joint Committee to the Economic Report, *Historical and Descriptive Supplement to Economic Indicators* (Washington, D.C.: U.S. Government Printing Office, 1953), p. 51.

9. Theodore W. Schultz, *Agriculture in an Unstable Economy* (New York: McGraw-Hill Book Company, Inc., 1945), pp. 171–172.

QUESTIONS

1. Explain why the federal government paid farmers to not plant or to plow up their crops. Was there any other possible solution to the farm problem?

2. Was Wallace paying farmers to do anything that differed in principle from what industry was doing by laying off workers?

3. Evaluate the success of Roosevelt's farm policy in light of the statistics found on pages 104 and 105.

SUGGESTED READING

John Stover depicts farm conditions and the politics of the Farm Holiday Association in *Cornbelt Rebellion* (Urbana: University of Illinois Press, 1965). Murray R. Benedict surveys agricultural policies during the New Deal in *Farm Policies of the United States, 1790–1950: A Study of Their Origins and Development* (New York: 20th Century Fund, 1953) and Russell Lord provides a highly informative anecdotal account in *The Wallaces of Iowa* (Boston: Houghton Mifflin Company, 1947). Thomas G. Manning and David Potter provide documents that allow students to shape their own analysis in *Government and the American Economy, 1870–Present* (New York: Henry Holt, 1950).

Chapter 13
The Farm Security Administration

Introduction

The Agricultural Adjustment Act was designed to raise farm incomes by government price supports and acreage reduction. This program, however, aided only those farmers with enough acreage and equipment to raise a fair-sized cash crop. AAA benefits gave little assistance to small farmers harvesting a tiny crop on a few sad acres. Many of these were tenant farmers operating perhaps twenty acres owned by their landlords. Except for the work of the Farm Security Administration, the small farmer almost became the forgotten man of the New Deal. This chapter traces the FSA's efforts to assist these less fortunate farmers who did not have a "family-size farm."*

Families living on inadequate farms that could not properly support a family were frequently caught in a vicious circle of a one-crop system, high interest charges, and limited skills. The FSA attacked all three problems simultaneously: through loans to improve farms or to purchase new ones; through diversified crops, including garden products for family self-support; and through the teaching of those skills necessary to plan and manage larger agricultural enterprises. The close government supervision and high administrative costs seemingly necessary to manage this kind of program became prime targets for attack by FSA's critics. FSA was accused of forcing loans on farmers and usurping their rights to make independent decisions. The entire program impressed some as merely a waste of time or money and others as a dangerous extension of government power over people's lives. This chapter presents debates over the need for the FSA and the merits or defects of charges levied against it.

---

*A family-size farm is one that gives a competent and industrious family an opportunity to get above the minimum standard for health and decency.

Croppers and Tenants

> Last year A.D. and his family produced seven bales of cotton which sold for
> $338.74. His share of the receipts was $169.37. But the landlord's books
> showed that A.D. owed him $184.12 and was, therefore, in debt $14.75. . . .
>
> A.D. had received no money from the government for soil-conservation
> crops. He hardly knew whether he had "cooperated," for as usual he and the
> other sharecroppers planted what they were told to plant. But a new tractor
> was bought, several fields were sown in peas and soy beans, and three of last
> year's tenant cabins were vacant—fewer workers needed.[1]

A.D. was a sharecropper. Like 716,000 other "cropper" families he
owned neither farm equipment, nor house, mule, or land. He had no cash,
no stocks, no bank account. Every spring he borrowed cash at 10 percent
interest to finance his crop. Every fall, after the harvest, he settled his account with his landlord, who also ran the only store in which A.D.'s credit
was good. After repaying his loans plus 10 percent interest and his bill at
the store, like most croppers A.D. usually found himself a little more in
debt. Average cropper income in 1935 was $71 per person or 20 cents a day.

Sharecroppers were among the lower quarter of America's farm population, living in dire poverty. Their homes were unpainted and dilapidated
two- or three-room shacks, with no proper sanitary facilities, no running
water, and no electricity. Since their diets were poor, they were prone to
disease, despondency, and early death. They had no extra money for doctor bills. Few attended church; they often did not have suitable or adequate
clothing, and schooling competed with planting, harvesting, and hoeing.
Their lives were drab and dreary with few pleasures and no luxuries.

According to one government report, *Farm Tenancy* (1937), 42 percent
of all farmers were tenants; that is, they rented rather than owned farms,
some 2,865,000 in all including the 716,000 "croppers." Most of these tenant farmers belonged to the 33 percent engaged in agriculture earning less
than 8 percent of the total farm income. In 1880, only 25 percent were
tenants. Since 1880, more and more farmers had lost their property every
year. Some left for the city:

> So I looked at my cotton receipts and my debt and I said, "A.D., you's goin'
> to town; you had a good year, but you ain't got nothin' and you never will
> have nothin' as long as you stay here." So me and my old lady and the chillun
> jes' lef'. No suh, I ain't got nothin' but some kin folks here and I ain't found
> them yet, but I's through with farmin'. Through. Yes sir, through.[2]

But millions, unlike A.D., clung to the poverty of the farm rather than
risk the prospect of poverty in the city.

The Causes of Rural Poverty

What did the federal government do to help these tenant farmers who
lived in poverty far worse than that of most who owned their own farms?
Very little under the Agriculture Adjustment Act of 1933, for while benefit
payments were made to landlords, few owners shared those windfalls with

(Farm Security Agency)

Living conditions among the rural poor became progressively more severe as the Depression deepened. People lost hope in their chance of holding on.

their tenants. Where the law requiring sharing might be enforced, tenants were simply evicted and perhaps re-hired as farm laborers for an hourly wage. Tenants did benefit by a rise in farm prices. But how beneficial were these increases when the tenant farmer sold only a few hundred dollars worth of commodities each year? Forty-seven percent of all farmers received only 11 percent of all government payments. Meanwhile, wealthier farmers, using AAA benefit payments to buy machinery that reduced their need for labor, evicted tenants when their work was no longer required.

Clearly, the causes of farm poverty lay much deeper than low prices. Many farmers were poor in prosperous times and their poverty could be

(Farm Security Agency)

Rather than starve on the farm Americans took to the road looking for work. Living out of a truck became a way of life for millions.

attributed partially to poor lands, partially to poor equipment, and partially to poor abilities. Landlords, moreover, demanded cash crops, not vegetable gardens. Conditions grew worse as housing deteriorated, as fields lost their fertility, and as malnutrition sapped the family's vitality. No bank would lend the poor farmer money to start anew, for he was a bad credit risk. A lifetime of scratching a miserable livelihood out of a few sorry acres prepared the farmer for nothing better and killed his hope.

The Farm Security Administration

Many of Roosevelt's advisors were concerned about farm poverty and established the Resettlement Administration in 1933 to remedy the situation. The low-income farmer was also to have his New Deal.* After some fumbling starts, resettlement projects were turned over to the newly established Farm Security Administration under the guidance of C. B. Baldwin. Baldwin handled a wide variety of programs, which are explained below.

1. Rehabilitation of farmers renting or owning land but unable to obtain

---

*FSA estimated that in 1929 on farms yielding less than $600 gross income (including debt-ridden small owner-farmers as well as tenant farmers) there were "approximately 7,700,000 men, women, and children" disadvantaged by "lack of purchasing power." *1940 Yearbook of Agriculture,* p. 889.

credit from private sources or from other government agencies. This program operated through loans and grants, supplemented by close supervision. Its purpose was to make farmers self-sustaining. It helped its recipients plan and market their cash crops, plan vegetable gardens, and learn to make their own canned products for winter use. It helped farmers meet some of their producing and marketing problems by arranging for the cooperative ownership of tractors, warehouses, and breeding stock. In addition, it assisted them in widening community participation by paying membership dues for farm organizations and by paying poll taxes. It even organized countywide group medical plans and worked with landlords to get better terms for tenants.

2. Resettlement mortgages to families, also unable to obtain other credit, for buying farms. Payments could be stretched over a forty-year period and were adjusted downward when poor harvests made repayment difficult. Tenant farmers ambitious to buy farms received some of this aid.

3. A program to improve conditions of migrant farm workers by building both permanent and mobile housing units for use during the harvest.

Accomplishments of the FSA

Because of the wide variety of programs under the Farm Security Administration, it is possible to give only some brief statistics covering FSA's accomplishments through 1941, its last full year of operation. Almost 1.5 million farmers were lent an average of $500 and 80 percent of these loans were considered repayable, leaving an expected defaulting ratio of only 20 percent; a bit surprising since FSA clients could not get credit elsewhere. Cash income of loan recipients, according to FSA estimates, increased by one-third, while net ownership increased by one-fifth and the value of goods produced increased 62 percent.

Farm mortgages under FSA averaged $5600, and 97 percent of these farmers repaid FSA. While 15,000 families were given help to buy farms, twenty times that number were refused application because of insufficient funds. In addition to helping buy farms, FSA built over 10,000 farmhouses for new owners.

Accommodations for over 15,000 migrant workers were built, in addition to numerous portable tent platform and kitchen units that could follow migrants as they moved from state to state.

FSA meant more to families than can be conveyed by statistics. For A.D. and his family it could have meant a new start in life, a chance for decent living conditions, self-respect, and opportunity for the children. For the many who were actually reached by FSA it meant that and more.

FSA in Coffey County

Coffey County, Alabama, had been struck by twin disasters. During the Depression, nearly one-half of the tillable land had been foreclosed. In addition, 60 percent of the school children either had hookworm or were suffering from other nutritional deficiencies. In 1936, FSA and other agencies began salvage operations. Six years later Dr. M. L. Wilson of the Department of Agriculture reported on the improvement:

(Farm Security Agency)

Migrants were a problem to the community—one that the sheriff usually handled. Here they are told to get off the road or get moving.

I visited a number of them [farmers helped by FSA] and in every case I was greatly impressed with the progress that each family was making with the home-grown food supplies that they had, and with the assistance of the health department . . . that practically all hookworm had been wiped out. As you go through the country and compare the status of the people now with what they were 5 or 6 years ago, I just think I can see them made over again. . . .

Now, I said to . . . the man who is in charge of the farm security project there . . . I want to stop at the next rehabilitation farm that we would come to. I did not want to be shown the best.

Well, we stopped at the next . . . farm and the farmer was a man who had completely lost his farm through foreclosure in 1934 or 1935. . . . He had first had a rehabilitation loan, then he had been placed on this farm. . . .

The wife took me out to show me her chickens. She had a brooder and had 250 little chicks that she had gotten from the hatchery.

The little boy, who was a member of the 4-H Club there, took me out and showed me his steer calf that he was taking into a 4-H Club show. . . . That was his calf. He had raised the calf and he had fattened the calf.

That family had a wonderfully good garden. They had, as I remember it, four or five cows. . . . They were entirely up with their payments.

Now, I would say, Senator, that their heads were up. There are not any better American citizens anywhere than that family. . . .

I think there are about 200 families in that county who have had rehabilitation loans . . . whose condition has been very greatly improved.[3]

Criticism of the FSA

The Farm Security Administration was changing living conditions for poor farmers, but not everyone wanted the government to be an agent of reform. Numerous criticisms of FSA were heard in all parts of the country where it operated.

(Farm Security Agency)

Erie, Pennsylvania, 1941–Busted farm families were relocated in this
FSA mobile home community–near their jobs in the new defense plant.

Some complained that FSA was forcing loans on people who had no
hope of repaying them, in order to keep them permanently indebted.

One farmer complained his FSA supervisor made him pay $50 for a cow
his former landlord preferred to lend him or sell to him for $36.

Senators Byrd of Virginia and McKellar of Tennessee were shocked to
discover FSA paid $36 in back poll taxes to qualify an FSA farmer for vot-
ing. Most poor farmers did not or could not vote in the states represented
by Byrd and McKellar, neither of whom wanted to abolish the poll tax.

One report stated that an FSA official made a farmer buy a chicken
brooder, but never provided the promised chickens because FSA mis-
placed the correct order blanks. Others reported digging wells which they
couldn't use because FSA officials were unable to find order blanks for
pumps. Some said FSA sold them hay at unreasonable prices.

Complaints were heard that FSA made grants to recipients who could
repay FSA loans for the sole purpose of making the administration's collection record look successful.

A quite opposite type of complaint was the accusation that FSA cooperative projects were socialistic. Some believed FSA was patterning projects after Russian collective farms. An FSA official was quoted as advocating subdividing large landholdings.

City folk wondered whether placing farmers back on the land was good
policy, especially when the government simultaneously was paying other
farmers not to produce. Others thought it inconsistent for the government
to finance farmers but not spend money to put people into businesses and
teach them how to run them.

Edward O'Neal, president of the powerful American Farm Bureau Fed-

eration, which represented big farmers, held rural rehabilitation to be unnecessary since AAA and industrial recovery could adequately help
farmers.

Some were merely opposed to spending the money, especially after
World War II started.

The American Farm Bureau, speaking for wealthier farmers, pointed out
that FSA spent one dollar on administration for every two dollars lent or
given away. But FSA director C. B. Baldwin denied these charges and dem-
onstrated that the Farm Bureau's estimate included many programs not
connected with FSA loans. He also showed that the Farm Bureau figured
only money lent each year rather than loans serviced during each year. The
ratio of administrative expenses to loans outstanding, Baldwin boasted,
was closer to 1:7.5, and this included close supervision of each loan. The
Farm Bureau also claimed FSA was lending money to help farmers join a
rival organization of small farmers, the Farmer's Union.

Based on the recommendations of its powerful enemies, the Farm Security Administration was phased out of existence during World War II. Some
believed its passing the end of a dangerous trend toward federal regulation;
others thought the government was turning its back on the federal responsibility to help the men who needed it most. Since that time the problems of the tenant and the unproductive farmer have remained unsolved,
although recently some programs have again been started to help men like
A.D.* There are public leaders and citizens, today, who feel that struggling
rural families have a right to farm and that the government has an obligation to support that right.

---

*The anti-poverty program today helps tenant farmers obtain loans.

NOTES

1. Arthur Raper and Ira De A Ried, *Sharecroppers All* (Chapel Hill: University of North
Carolina Press, 1941), pp. 63–64.

2. *Ibid.,* p. 64.

3. United States Congress, Senate, Committee on Appropriations, *Agricultural Appropriations Bill, 1943,* hearings before subcommittee, 77th Congress, 2nd Session, on H.R. 6709
(Washington, D.C.: U.S. Government Printing Office, 1943), p. 958.

QUESTIONS

1. Are the sharecroppers (like A.D.) and poor tenant farmers victims of
circumstances beyond their control or do they have mostly themselves to
blame for their economic condition? Explain.

2. Should it be the federal government's responsibility to help tenant farmers and sharecroppers? Why or why not?

3. Do programs like the FSA tend to lead to dangerous increases in federal
power and to wasting federal money? Does the evidence against FSA warrant this charge? Explain.

SUGGESTED READING

For the condition of the sharecroppers see: Walker Evans and James Agee, *Let Us Now Praise Famous Men* (Boston: Houghton Mifflin Company, 1960), Margaret Bourke-White and Erskine Caldwell, *You Have Seen Their Faces* (New York: Viking Press, 1937), and Arthur Raper and Ira De A Ried, *Sharecroppers All* (Chapel Hill: University of North Carolina Press, 1941). In *Revolt Among the Sharecroppers* (New York: Arno Press and the *New York Times,* 1969), Howard Kister describes the living conditions of the croppers and an interracial movement among the dispossessed to improve their lot.

Chapter 14

Social Security : Insurance or Welfare

Introduction

When the federal government gave aid to farmers, the cost of the program was met out of general tax funds as was the cost of WPA. But when President Roosevelt asked Congress to legislate permanent aid programs (Social Security) for the aged, unemployed, and unemployables, the funds to pay for these programs were to come directly from the beneficiaries. Because the workers and their employers were taxed in this fashion, Social Security was a self-supporting program. However, because it is self-supporting, Social Security is not as complete as it might have been if financed directly from general taxes. This chapter examines the advantages of both methods of taxation.

The Cornerstone

In late July, 1965, President Lyndon Baines Johnson traveled to Independence, Missouri, to sign the Medicare Bill at the home of former President Harry Truman. Johnson made this special trip because Truman had originally proposed a medical insurance plan 20 years before. In a speech during the ceremony, Johnson honored yet a third president, Franklin D. Roosevelt, who had been responsible for establishing the Social Security System in 1935 and who characterized it as "a cornerstone in the structure which is being built but is by no means complete."[1]

The cornerstone to which Roosevelt had referred was a minimum of security protecting a group (the aged, the unemployed, and the unemployables) who were unable to care for themselves. By paying for hospital and doctor care for citizens age 65 and over, the Medicare Bill extended the scope of assistance of the Social Security Act of 1935.

Three Parts of the Social Security Program

Under the program established by Roosevelt in 1935 and extended under every succeeding president, three forms of coverage were provided. The first form, known as Old Age, Survivors and Disability Insurance (OASDI), is the most familiar because it takes 4.2 percent of the pay check. Benefits are paid to retired or disabled workers, their widows or orphaned children, but actual payments vary according to the amount contributed. Since nearly all workers contribute to OASDI, everyone eventually becomes eligible for benefits. Even if the worker doesn't live long enough to collect, his wife or children usually do. Under the Medicare bill of 1965, most hospital and doctor bills for the aged are also paid (including those for people not eligible for Social Security).*

Unemployment compensation is also connected with Social Security. The worker waiting for his unemployment check will actually collect money contributed by his and other employers for these emergencies. Benefits vary according to the state and the weekly wages of the worker. Though state unemployment offices administer this program, the federal government sets certain minimum standards.

Aid to poor and needy individuals, including the blind, the disabled, and dependent children and their mothers, forms the third major social security program. Here people are given assistance even if they have not contributed, for help is given on the basis of need. All other parts of the social security program are financed by payroll deductions.

Social Security Based on the Insurance Principle

The Social Security System was established on much the same principles as private insurance. Where private insurance companies bill their customers, the federal government collects payments from workers or their employers; the significant difference is that Social Security contributions, like taxes, are compulsory. Under both public and private insurance, a reserve fund is established which recipients draw upon when they become eligible. Contributions therefore must be steep enough to guarantee a reserve sufficient to meet all claims. Today the OASDI account contains over $20 billion, and benefits are paid to 22 million Americans. Approximately 110 million workers contribute to this fund. Increased benefits naturally must be financed by higher payments. That is why Social Security taxes have risen from no more than $30 a year in 1936 to $277 a year in 1966. And that is why they will continue to climb.

Social Security did not have to be financed according to the insurance principle. Before the program was introduced in 1935, many people felt benefits should be financed by income and inheritance taxes. This would tax the individuals best able to pay while yielding enough money to in-

---

*To pay for these additional benefits, Social Security payroll taxes will be raised to 5.6 percent of the first $6600 of income. Employers are required to match this payroll tax dollar for dollar. The total yearly tax on $6600 therefore comes to $755.80.

Michigan, 1935–This man and woman farmed in Oklahoma until they lost their land–then became agricultural day laborers–finally migrants. This was taken in their home of the moment–an abandoned farmhouse near where they were working picking fruit. What is ahead for them?

crease benefit payments. It was argued that a program paid out of such taxes would charge the wealthy, who could afford to give, and help the poor, who needed it most; or, as opponents of this proposal put it, charge the industrious to benefit the lazy and shiftless. Since sentiment for financing social security through general taxation still persists, this chapter examines some clashing arguments concerning the welfare and insurance principles.

The Argument for Insurance

For almost 150 years, no state in the union had any kind of a social security system, nor did the federal government make provisions for helping the unemployed or the aged. Many reasons can explain this failure, but the most important are connected with a belief in the need for initiative and thrift. The unemployed were expected to look for work rather than loaf. What makes a worker actively seek employment but the need for food and shelter? Provide the unemployed with money payments and he will have no incentive or initiative to take a job. Guarantee the laborer a comfortable pension and he will not save money to provide for his retirement. Destroy both thrift and initiative and you have neither savings nor workers; neither money to invest nor employees to toil. Help for the aged and the unemployed is therefore false charity; you assist the individual and by so doing destroy his incentive and the entire system of production and distribution on which his well-being is based.

Millions were unemployed during the Depression and consequently billions in savings were destroyed through no fault of the suffering idle. Therefore, in the name of humanity, restrictions on aiding the unemployed and the aged were relaxed. But how does one act charitably if charity destroys its object?

The answer was to provide assistance in small doses so as to avoid destroying the incentive to work or to save; and, as a further safeguard, to help only responsible workers willing and able to contribute to their own welfare. The insurance principle provides these safeguards. It limits workers' benefits in accordance with the days they toiled and the moneys they contributed. It eliminates aid to workers who have loafed in the past and therefore did not contribute to the fund. It prevents taxing the "industrious" to aid the "shiftless."

The program developed under this philosophy is described below. It was designed not to prevent depressions, but to establish a minimum floor of security for the responsible worker. It could not help the already unemployed because they hadn't contributed toward its establishment. And it provided maximum freedom for individual states to experiment with programs of their own.

The Social Security Act of 1935

The Social Security program adopted in 1935 was based on Roosevelt's recommendation that Congress adhere to sound insurance principles. The Act provided for the following:

1. *A monthly pension of $10 to $85 for retired workers over 65 who had contributed a portion of their wages for each of five calendar years and who paid on over $2000 of minimum income.* So that a reserve could be built up first, payments were not to start until 1942. To simplify administration of this program, agricultural workers, domestics or servants, those working in small businesses employing less than 8, and the self-employed were not included. About 50 percent of all workers were covered in this part of the program.

2. *A 3 percent payroll tax to be collected by the federal government and returned to the states if they established a program of unemployment insurance.* Before 1940, all forty-eight states established such a program, with benefits usually starting after the fourth week of unemployment and lasting till the sixteenth. Weekly insurance payments were not to exceed 50 percent of the worker's salary, but were limited to a maximum of $18 and a minimum of $5.

3. *Various forms of assistance to the disabled, crippled, and aged, rang-ing in kind from supplementary pensions based on need to moneys granted states for improving health facilities and to offers of medical assistance for needy mothers.*

The Argument for Welfare

Many Americans who would actually live on social security were seri-ously disturbed by what they considered the inadequate benefits of Roosevelt's program. The idea of insurance was completely wrong, they believed, for no program under the insurance system could provide suffi-cient benefits. The most needy were without either work or savings and therefore were least able to afford contributing to the system. Further-more, they needed more than $10 a month upon retirement or $5 a week when unemployed. These sums could barely sustain life, much less provide a healthy standard of living, even with the comparatively low prices of the 1930's.

The pittance provided by insurance also failed to maintain purchasing power. The cause of the Depression, some argued, was found in the fail-ure of purchasing power to keep pace with productivity. Unemployed or retired workers with little or no money could not spend, and their inability

SOCIAL SECURITY PAYMENTS, BY CATEGORY, 1965

*I. Old-Age, Survivors, and Disability Insurance,
    Average Monthly Payments*

Retired worker	$ 80.89
Wife or husband of retired worker	39.58
Widow or widower of retired worker	73.68
Parent of retired worker	80.46
Child of retired worker	29.18
Child of deceased worker	53.19
Widowed mother	59.22
Disabled worker	93.66
Wife or husband of disabled worker	34.26
Child of disabled worker	28.20

II. Unemployment Insurance

Average weekly benefit for unemployed worker	$ 36.40
Lowest average payment	22.86
Highest average payment	44.09

III. Public Assistance, Average Monthly Payment

Old-age assistance	$ 79.69
Aid to the blind	86.43
Medical assistance to the aged	191.65
Aid to the permanently disabled	83.49
Aid to families with dependent children, per child	34.02
General assistance	30.88

Source: Social Security Bulletin, September, 1965, vol. 28 number 9, pp. 35, 37, 38, 39.

to buy caused business to stop investing and producing. When industry threw more workers off their jobs, a vicious cycle began that could only be broken by re-establishing purchasing power. Prosperity would return when either work or income was restored. A public works program could accomplish the former and social welfare would guarantee the latter.

One way of financing these programs would be to tax the rich who could afford paying and, in any case, saved a good portion of their incomes. Thus the government would play Robin Hood, taxing the wealthy who tended to save and giving to the poor who tended to spend.

The Lundeen or Worker's Bill

Originally the Communist party sponsored the social security program based on the welfare idea. But it also gained devoted support from a large number of non-Communist social workers and labor leaders. The bill was introduced to Congress by Representative Ernest Lundeen. Its major provisions are outlined below:

1. Men or women, including the aged and disabled, unable to find work for any reason whatsoever, are to be paid a weekly salary equal to the average weekly earnings for their kind of work, and never less than $10 plus $3 a dependent.

2. The money to pay for this program will come from taxes on individual or corporation incomes above $5 thousand, on gifts, and on inheritances.

3. Councils of workers and farmers will supervise the distribution of this money.

The chart below compares the two bills on several important points.

	Lundeen	*Roosevelt*
Who is covered	All men and women unable to find work.	About 50 percent of all workers; farmers, domestics, self-employed, etc., are not included.
Extent of benefits	Worker's average weekly earning, but never less than $10 week + $3 a dependent. Benefits will start immediately.	Retired workers paid $10–$85 per month, starting in 1942. Unemployed will receive 50 percent of wages for 12 weeks after the 4th week of unemployment, but never more than $18. Program starts in 1938.
Who pays	Program financed through taxes on inheritance, gifts, and corporate or private incomes above $5 thousand.	Retirement plan—3% deducted from first $3 thousand wages and same deducted from employer. Unemployment insurance—3% deducted from payrolls.
Who administers program	Councils of farmers and workers.	Retired get money from federal government through Social Security office. Unemployed get money from states through unemployment office.
Cost to taxpayer	At least 10 million eligible, cost $200 million a week until unemployment slackens.	Nothing, since bill financed completely through contributions from workers and employers.

Ernest Lundeen's efforts to have Congress adopt his proposals were blocked by the President, who put the prestige of his office behind the bill based on insurance, not welfare. Congress, with Roosevelt's approval, rejected the Lundeen bill when it was offered as an amendment to replace the more conservative Social Security measure. But Congress's decision did not completely end the debate over basing Social Security on welfare rather than insurance. As Social Security taxes continue mounting (combined employer-employee contributions will take 11.3 percent of an employee's Social Security base pay by 1987) and as Social Security coverage continues to expand, many students of Social Security advocate supplementing payroll deductions with funds from general taxation. Thus the welfare principle may yet be introduced in the Social Security system.

NOTE

1. *New York Times,* July 31, 1965, p. 9.

QUESTIONS

1. Should the federal government help the aged, unemployed, or the unemployables?

2. Should this program take the form of forced insurance or welfare?

3. Criticize specific aspects of Roosevelt's or Lundeen's plan with reference to effects on incentive, purchasing power, and recipient's standard of living.

SUGGESTED READING

Paul H. Douglas explains the Lundeen bill in *Social Security in the United States* (New York: McGraw-Hill Book Company, Inc., 1936). Other works on the Social Security Act include Edwin E. Witte, *Development of the Social Security Act* (Madison: University of Wisconsin Press, 1962), and Evaline Burns, *Toward Social Security: An Explanantion of the Social Security Act and a Summary of the Larger Issues* (New York: McGraw-Hill Book Company, Inc., 1936).

Chapter 15
Protecting the Investor

Introduction

When the stock market crash of October, 1929, occurred, Wall Street was operating with virtually no government regulation other than ineffective state laws that did not protect the investor. According to the economic theories of Andrew Mellon and conservative businessmen, the mainspring of economic health was private investment. Yet Mellon and the business community were so opposed to federal regulation of anything that they could see no reason for legislation to protect investors. The interests of the investor, they argued, would be protected by the wise men who actually ran the stock market, its Board of Governors. No government agency could possibly acquire the detailed knowledge needed to control the stock exchange, and regulation of securities would only succeed in driving the stock market into Canada. This chapter covers the battle to extend government regulation to the stock exchange and the practices which seemed to necessitate protection for investors. The reader will be asked to decide whether investors, like farmers and the aged, needed government protection.

Edgar Brown's Faith in National City Bank

For reasons of health, Edgar Brown of Pottsville, Pennsylvania, sold his chain of theaters for $100 thousand and in 1927 prepared a move to California. While looking for a safe place to invest his savings, Brown spied a magazine advertisement advising investors to consult a National City Bank representative. Believing this bank to be the nation's soundest, Brown answered the ad. Fred Rummel, a salesman for the bank's affiliate, the National City Company, called on Brown and persuaded him to borrow money and buy not $100 thousand but $250 thousand worth of foreign bonds, including a large number from Peru. Neither Rummel nor the investment brochures informed Brown that National City Company's vice-president had recently advised his home office that Peru was a poor credit

risk as the political situation there was unstable and presented few opportunities for economic growth.

Realizing he was losing money on his foreign bonds, Brown again con-
tacted Rummel, who then sold him stock in National City Bank and Anaconda Copper Corporation. Again Brown was the victim of inadequate
information, for Rummel did not tell him that copper prices had recently
fallen by 25 percent. Nor did Rummel bother telling his customer that National City was trying to unload 300 thousand shares of Anaconda.

Brown also remained ignorant of a rather cozy financial relationship
between the National City Bank and Anaconda. The director of Anaconda
was a member of National City's board, and Anaconda, naturally, did
its banking at National City. Furthermore, Brown did not know that both
National City Bank and National City Company were run by Board Chairman Charles E. Mitchell. Indeed, Mitchell ran the two corporations like
one firm; the first handled banking functions and the second issued and
sold securities. The bank, as a matter of fact, actually owned the company.
Had Brown known this, he might have wondered why these two firms were
listed as separate organizations. The answer was relatively simple: banks
were not allowed to speculate in securities, but no law prohibited the National City Bank from owning an "investment house." Had Brown realized
National City Company's profits would end up in the National City Bank,
he might well have gone elsewhere for confidential, objective, and dis-
interested investment advice.

When Brown's bank and mining stock proved to be a poor investment,
he visited a National City Company branch office in California, on October
4, 1929, to request sale of his holdings. There he was treated like a "man
who seeks to put his mother out of his house"[1] and was told that "that was
a very, very foolish thing to do."[2] Three and one-half weeks later, Brown
wished his sales resistance was somewhat stronger, for the crash came and
he was among the thousands of small investors who were completely
ruined. His National City Bank stock fell over $500, to $21 a share. Per-
uvian bonds sold for 4 5/8 in 1933, and Anaconda stock did almost as
badly. In 1933, his savings completely lost, Edgar Brown was clerking for
Pottsville's poor board, back in Pennsylvania.

National City's "Management Fund"

At the New York headquarters of the National City Bank, a most un-
usual ritual took place every January and June. The bank's president,
Charles Mitchell, and his many vice-presidents would each evaluate the
work performed by their fellow executives. They did this by assigning a
certain share of the bank's money to each other. This reshuffling of the
bank's wealth was done by writing a number on a piece of paper and drop-
ping it into a box. Mitchell would tabulate the evaluation of each executive
and pay him from a special account called the "management fund." A full
20 percent of the bank's profits would be distributed in this way, and Mitchell's share alone over a 3-year period amounted to almost $3.5 million.
National City's stockholders were paid only after her top executives received their "management fund."

DRASTIC STOCK MARKET BILL PROVIDES FEDERAL CONTROL; OUTLAWS 9 TYPES OF DEALS

INTRODUCED IN CONGRESS

President, in Special Message, Urges Curb on 'Naked Speculation.'

BILL SETS MARGIN AT 60%

But Buyer Has Alternative of Credit of 80% of Lowest Price in Three Years.

TRADE BOARD TO CONTROL

Short Selling, Wash Sales, Proxies and Option Trading Regulated.

Stock Exchange Bill, Pages 6, 7. President's message Page 6 and Fletcher's speech, Page 7.

Special to THE NEW YORK TIMES.
WASHINGTON, Feb. 9.—President Roosevelt in a special message today asked for legislation to regulate stock exchanges and immediately the long-awaited bill was introduced in Senate and House. It proved to be one of the most drastic re???? ??? ??? ???

Chief Points of Stock Exchange Bill

Special to THE NEW YORK TIMES.

WASHINGTON, Feb. 9.—*The principal provisions of the Fletcher-Rayburn Stock Exchange Regulation Bill, introduced in Congress today, are as follows:*

Requires registration of stock exchanges as "national securities exchanges" with the Federal Trade Commission, the agency administering the proposed law.

Makes it a criminal offense to manipulate security prices on exchanges, the devices outlawed including pools, wash sales, spreading of rumors of impending price changes, cornering the supply of a security and pegging prices without informing the Trade Commission of all details of the transaction.

Stipulates 60 per cent of current prices as a margin requirement, but gives to a trader the option of covering his share purchase with credit up to 80 per cent of the lowest quotation on the security within the three preceding years.

Authorizes the Trade Commission to require annual, quarterly and monthly reports on financial condition from corporations whose stocks are registered on exchanges.

Prohibits short selling or stop loss orders and "over-the-counter" market transactions unless authorized by and in compliance with regulations of the Trade Commission.

Imposes a fine not to exceed $25,000 or imprisonment for not more than ten years for violation of any provision of the law by an individual and a fine not to exceed $500,000 for violation by an exchange.

STOCKS OFF 1 TO 3 ON NEWS OF BILL

Then They Rally When President Fails to Endorse the Fletcher Measure.

VIENNA FOES UNITE AGAINST HEIMWEHR

Clerical Deputies Join With the Socialists in Diet to Fight Demands for Dictatorship.

This unique profit-sharing plan undoubtedly affected the performance of National City's managers. Before a Senate investigating committee probing into this practice, Charles Mitchell argued that the management fund established an "esprit de corps" among his executives. Senator Couzens asked Mitchell if this spirit wouldn't tend to make the executives forget the welfare of their customers, and lead to carelessness in "handling the sale of securities to the public." "I can readily see, from your point of view, that it would seem so," Mitchell replied, "[but] I do not recall seeing it operate that way."[3]

"Pools" Defraud Speculators

Even more ignorant than the naive investor were those brazen souls who thought they could beat the big-time market operators at their own game. Consider the case of the man buying Radio Corporation stock in 1928. Chapter 4 showed how one group of operators had been helped by stock specialist Michael J. Meehan. Meehan and his friends formed a pool which bought and sold radio stocks until the public, sensing fantastic profits, was pulled in. Such stock manipulation created the illusion of easy money, which in reality was not based on the solid growth of the industry these stocks represented. The radio illusion lasted for 18 months until the inevitable sobering facts smashed the pretense and the market.

Before 1934, no federal law prevented insiders from artificially pushing stocks up by buying and selling among themselves. Only the threat of public exposure and the consequent fear of financial loss or disgrace prevented such activity. These were frail restraints indeed when measured against the temptation of huge profits. In truth, the New York Stock Exchange prohibited this practice, but seldom punished it. A flurry of activity in alcohol stocks and a subsequent Senate investigation employing Ferdinand Pecora as counsel illustrates this point.

Between May 2, and July 18, 1933, American Commercial Alcohol Corporation stock climbed spectacularly from $20 to $79 a share. During the next three days, Alcohol's entire gain was lost in a wave of selling orders. Coincidence? Not according to the suprisingly frank testimony of Charles C. Wright, specialist in American Alcohol stock:

> *Mr. Pecora:* In addition to getting discretionary orders* to sell, did you also get during that period of time discretionary verbal orders from Bragg to buy?
>
> *Mr. Wright:* Yes, sir.
>
> *Mr. Pecora:* Could you tell the committee from your recollection or, if not from your recollection, from any records available now, what was the largest discretionary order either to buy or to sell American Commercial Alcohol stock that Bragg gave you during the operation of that pool?
>
> *Mr. Wright:* . . . I would say that about the largest I remember was 5 thousand shares. . . .
>
> *Mr. Pecora:* I presume you frequently, during that period, got orders to both buy and sell from Bragg on the same date?
>
> *Mr. Wright:* Yes, sir. . . .
>
> *Mr. Pecora:* . . . When Bragg would give you a discretionary order to buy for his account, during the operation of the pool last summer, you believed from your instinct that he was buying in order to put the market up; you exercised that discretion for the purpose of putting the market up?
>
> *Mr. Wright:* Mr. Bragg does not work that way. When he gave me buying orders he gave me orders so that there would only be support in that stock. He didn't buy it up.
>
> *Mr. Pecora:* How would the higher levels be attained?
>
> *Mr. Wright:* By the natural desire of people at that particular time to trade in whiskey stocks. . . .[4]

---

*A discretionary order, as the term implies, allows the specialist to decide when to buy or sell the stock.

Subsequent testimony revealed that this Mr. Bragg had an option (right) to buy 25 thousand shares of American Commercial Alcohol Corporation stock at $18 per share, no matter how low or high the market. This option naturally was worth more when American Commercial sold for $79 than when it sold for $18, and Bragg was therefore encouraged to bid the stock up. Other market operators did the same, and they all contributed to this stock's sudden rise. After Bragg and these operators cashed in their options and sold them at inflated prices, they stopped supporting American Alcohol and the stock quickly descended to its earlier levels. Unwary investors who bought at $35 or more were victimized by the manipulators with the options.

The New York Stock Exchange Opposes Regulation

The New York Stock Exchange's history may be traced back to a group of merchants trading under the trees on Wall Street, New York, in 1791. Long before 1929, the market had moved indoors and was a vast network servicing brokers and buyers all over the world. But it never lost the atmosphere of a private and somewhat exclusive club of business associates. Only 1375 men were actually allowed to buy or sell stocks on the exchange and each paid a small fortune for that privilege.

The Exchange did have rules, which were administered by a 42-man Board of Governors elected by menbers. Richard Whitney, the man who temporarily saved the market in 1929 by his dramatic bid for U.S. Steel, was president of the Board. Whitney now feared the federal government would destroy the Exchange through excessive regulation, and he was prepared to fight this danger with every resource at his command.

The Public Demands Regulation of the Exchange

The demand for federal regulation of the stock market came from many sources. The excessive speculation of the 1920's led thoughtful citizens to feel the need for corrective action. Using the Senate Banking Committee as his forum, Ferdinand Pecora ruthlessly exposed the activities of operators like Michael J. Meehan and Charles E. Mitchell. Roosevelt met this demand for reform by urging federal regulation for issuing stocks, and regulation of the Exchange itself. Ultimately demands for reform were translated into three major laws: the Banking Act of 1933, the so-called "truth in securities" bill of 1933, and the Securities Exchange Act of 1934. The following list summarizes the major provisions of this legislation:

1. Banks could no longer own investment houses nor could anyone serve simultaneously as an officer in a bank and an investment firm. In other words, banks were limited to accepting deposits and making loans and investment houses were limited to issuing and selling securities.

2. The sellers of securities were held responsible and personally liable for all information given about the securities they sold.

3. Corporations were forced to reveal publicly all information pertinent to the stocks they issued, including revelation of persons or firms profiting from the sale of these stocks.

4. A five-man body, the Securities and Exchange Commission, was given power to regulate operations of the various stock exchanges in the nation

and enforce legislation concerning the exchange.

5. Manipulating security prices through pools or other means was out-lawed.

6. All members of the stock exchange had to publicize their financial affairs, particularly their market activities.

7. The federal government, through the Federal Reserve Board, could set margin requirements.

Richard Whitney Defends the Exchange

Richard Whitney personally directed the opposition to stock exchange legislation. Calling the market a "perfect" institution, Whitney warned that regulation would ruin the Exchange, for it would drive the buying and selling of stocks into Canada. The proposed legislation, Whitney claimed, would stop speculations, and yet "speculation was the thing that built this country."[5] Besides, the market could be regulated far more successfully by its Board of Governors, who Whitney thought had already taken steps to curb its excesses. The following testimony before the House Commerce Committee provides the reader with evidence to take into account in evaluating Whitney's arguments.

Mr. Wolverton: Do you feel that power should be lodged in individuals without responsibility other than that which they are willing to assume, or should it be placed in an authority that has responsibility to the people?

Mr. Whitney: Why, Mr. Wolverton, I thought I had answered you. To my way—

Mr. Wolverton: You answered, Mr. Whitney, to the extent of saying that you believed it should be left just as it is; but I would appreciate very much having the reasons that led you to that conclusion.

Mr. Whitney: Yes sir; I would like to give it if I knew how to answer you.

As I see it, that responsibility lies on the heads of those that take it in the first place, and lies on the heads of the individual in control of an operation such as an exchange, who have a far graver responsibility, to my mind, than if it lies upon the heads of a commission appointed under an act.

I cannot conceive by any stretch of the imagination how any commission could have been informed of the facts, could have had time to have gone into details; in particular in the technical matters in which I do not believe any administrative body could have the information, or experience, as compared with what members of the governing committee have in order to take such action with the promptness that such action warrants.

Mr. Wolverton: Then it is your thought that it would be impossible for any government agency to be set up that to be as keenly appreciative of their responsibility or have the knowledge that you, as a private member of the stock exchange might have, and that would enable them to act . . .

Mr. Whitney: No sir; I think that they would be fully as appreciative of their responsibility; . . .

Mr. Wolverton: So then the people of the nation, then, are absolutely dependent on the good faith of the individuals who control the stock exchange?

Mr. Whitney: In such matters; yes, sir.

Mr. Wolverton: And there will be no way in which their rights could be preserved except by them depending upon the good intention and conscience of those who happen to occupy these particular positions?

Mr. Whitney: If I understand what you mean by their rights; yes, sir.[6]

But Whitney lost his argument and Congress passed their laws designed to curb the abuses of the 1920's and 1930's. The stock market is still in New York and going strong. Many still believe the need is now for more, rather than less regulation.

NOTES

1. Ferdinand Pecora, *Wall Street Under Oath* (New York: Simon and Schuster, 1939), p. 89.
2. *Ibid.*
3. *Ibid.,* p. 118.
4. United States Congress, Senate, Committee on Banking and Currency, *Stock Exchange Practices,* 73rd Congress, 2nd Session, on S: 84, S. 56, and S. 97, February 14–20, 1934, Part 13 (Washington, D.C.: U.S. Government Printing Office, 1934), pp. 6103–6104.
5. J. Woolf, "Whitney Defends the Takers of Risks," *New York Times Magazine,* July 3, 1932, p. 3.
6. United States Congress, House of Representatives, The Committee on Interstate and Foreign Commerce, *To Provide for Registration of National Securities . . . and Other Purposes,* 73rd Congress, 2nd Session, on H.R. 7852 and H.R. 8720, February 14–March 14, 1934 (Washington D.C.: U.S. Government Printing Office, 1934), pp. 195–197.

QUESTIONS

1. Should Edgar Brown, rather than the National City Bank, be blamed for his foolish investment?

2. Do the major provisions of the Banking Act, the "truth in securities" bill, and the Stock Exchange Act correct practices which need regulation? Explain your answer by evaluating each regulatory measure.

3. Carefully evaluate Whitney's arguments for self-regulation of the stock exchange in the light of the abuses during the period in which he presided over the exchange.

SUGGESTED READING

In *Wall Street Under Oath* (New York: Simon and Schuster, 1939), Ferdinand Pecora unfolds the dramatic testimony he unearthed in the famous Senate Banking Committee investigations. Frank Cornier brings the story of fraud on Wall Street up to date in *Wall Street's Shady Side* (Washington, D.C.: Public Affairs Press, 1962). Focusing on the crash of 1929 John G. Fuller uncovers further problems among the bankers in *The Money Changers* (New York: Dial Press, 1962). In *Wall Street, the Other Las Vegas* (New York: Lyle Stuart, 1964), Nicolas Darvas elaborates on the story originally chronicled in *How I Made Two Million Dollars in the Market.*

Chapter 16
Who Shall Pay ?
The Problem of Taxes

Introduction

J. P. Morgan paid no income taxes in 1930, 1931, or 1933. Neither did the majority of his partners; nor did many of the other richest men in America. They merely took advantage of loopholes in the revenue laws by establishing paper losses on stock sales to their wives or friends and repurchasing these securities soon after tax returns were filed. These men exercised skill at a game open only to the very rich.

In truth, no one really enjoys paying taxes. Taxes, however, have been defined as the price paid for civilization, because government cannot function without a source of income. Taxes pay the legislator, the policeman, the teacher, and the postman; without taxes there could be no law, no law enforcement, no education, no communication. Without taxes there would be no civilization.

Before the turn of the century, federal revenues were derived primarily from tariffs. Though a tax on incomes was levied and collected during the Civil War, the Supreme Court ruled the income tax unconstitutional in 1895, and only a constitutional amendment revived it in time to help finance World War I. Under Andrew Mellon's leadership in the 1920's, the high war-time rates were sharply reduced (see Chapter 1). The Depression years, which brought such drastic hardships to so many people, made the practice of income tax evasion by the wealthy seem all the more reprehensible. Popular resentment against the practice and against the rich themselves put pressure on Congress to revive the steep tax schedules of the World War I era. Moreover, high taxes were thought necessary to finance Roosevelt's New Deal programs and reduce annual deficits at a time when depression had shrunk government revenues. Roosevelt's administration was constructing public works projects, distributing relief, buying farm surpluses, paying old age benefits to the retired, and developing the Tennessee Valley. These new public services were expensive. The basic controversy was, who should pay for them and how much should they pay?

The President Proposes to Tax the Rich

Even in normal times, every class of people can find convincing arguments why it would be fairer or wiser to tax some other class. These arguments become the more heated because personal interest is usually coupled with predictions of a tax rate's disastrous effect on the national economic welfare. When high rates were proposed for the very rich (the J. P. Morgans and the Andrew Mellons) in order to redistribute or "share" their wealth, the tax debate became very hot. Imagine the reaction of millionaires in 1935 when Roosevelt advised Congress that:

> Great accumulations of wealth cannot be justified on the basis of personal and family security. In the last analysis such accumulations amount to the perpetuation of great and undesirable concentration of control in a relatively few individuals over the employment and welfare of many, many others. . . .
>
> The disturbing effects upon our national life that come from great inheritances of wealth and power can in the future be reduced . . . through a definite increase in the taxes now levied upon very great individual net incomes.[1]

The President then outlined a tax program that would reduce "accumulations of wealth" through steep individual taxes on high incomes and increased inheritance and gift taxes.

An Analysis of the Problem

While Roosevelt's message was cheered in the House of Representatives, it was met with a stony silence in the Senate and elicited an angry telegram from the San Francisco Chamber of Commerce: "Business activity, which should be encouraged as the source of the greatest possible revenue, would be deliberately and permanently throttled by the proposed ruthless confiscation of property."[2]

Formal hearings on the controversial tax proposal began in the House on July 8, 1935, and three weeks later in the Senate. But the ideas discussed were older than that Congress and as current as today's newspaper. For the sake of clarity, they are broken into three separate but interrelated topics:

1. *Justice:* Is it fair that A's yearly income is $500 while B receives $1 million? Should the government do something to equalize these earnings? But then is it fair that A is untouched by federal taxes while B pays more than half of his income to the government?

2. *Economic effect on incentive and purchasing power:* Will forcing B to pay high taxes destroy his desire to work or his incentive to invest, thereby preventing industrial expansion? Will failure to tax B leave him with more income than he can possibly spend, and reduce purchasing and production?

3. *Raise revenue:* Will higher taxes actually increase government revenues or will they depress business activity and yield less total tax than would a lower tax rate? Does tax reduction sometimes encourage production and increase the tax yield?

Congress Considers: 1. Justice

Redistribution of wealth through the tyrannical agency of taxation affronts every principle of sound Americanism and every established tenet of economics.[3]

—George B. Chandler, Secretary of Ohio Chamber of Commerce

. . . Even today . . . total income is still sufficient to maintain every family upon a decent level of life. The trouble is the total national income is now unwisely and inequitably distributed.[4]

—Rabbi Sidney Goldstein, Chairman, Commission of Social Justice

LaGuardia Wants a Progressive Income Tax to Redistribute Wealth

Mr. La Guardia: Now, the purpose of income tax law, a progressive income tax law, is not only to raise revenue. I stress that very strongly as a social measure to prevent concentration of wealth.

The purpose of inheritance taxes is not revenue primarily. Let us be frank about that, because unless we establish in this country high rates of inheritance tax within the next 25 or 30 years . . . most of the wealth of the country will be concentrated in a few families. . . .

Mr. Crisp: I thought possibly you might have—I have seen the statement made that 15 percent of the people of the United States own 90 percent of the wealth of the United States. . . .

Mr. LaGuardia: Oh, I put it at a much lower percentage than that. That 5 percent own 90 percent of the wealth.[5]

Marklan Thinks Wealth Is Already Well Distributed

George Marklan: Wealth is more equitably distributed in this country than anywhere else in the world. There are 22 million automobiles on the streets and highways of this country, and about 70 percent of the people who work have bathtubs, electric lights, and radios in their homes. . . .[6]

Chandler Says Redistribution Is Communistic

Mr. Chandler: . . . the most striking modern example . . . of redistribution of wealth is Soviet Russia. Here they have not redistributed it. They have simply taken it away and killed off its owners. Maybe some of the oily propagandists that are whispering around Washington think Russia a better country to live in than the United States. If so, the seas are open to them.[7]

Holman Wonders If Industries Should Be Taxed to Help the Shiftless

Senator Holman: . . . Are the thrifty and the self-denying, and the enterprising to be taxed on their labor to lead around by the hands the unthrifty and the shiftless, and so forth? I do not say that they are all unthrifty and shiftless. A lot of them are unfortunate; but there, the power to tax is the power to destroy, and if we tax the enterprise of the thrifty for the benefit of the improvident—of course those terms are too general, I know, but I think you get it. Do I make myself clear as to what is going on in my own mind?

(The New York Times)

The way it looks to a critic.

Many felt that Roosevelt's programs were anti-business, and that they prevented rather than promoted recovery.

Senator Aiken: Yes; and I think, theoretically, you are just right, . . . but the question then comes up, how do the thrifty happen to be affluent? Did they get affluent through their own thrift, or did they get affluent by being able to get the state or the federal legislature to enact legislation which gave them an unfair advantage over these less thrifty people who may be poor because of their own selfishness, or may be poor because somebody else has been getting the benefit of their labor all of the time?[8]

Marklan Doesn't Want to Support Incompetents

Mr. Marklan: We are attempting to tax people who work, who create wealth and distribute wealth—we are attempting to tax them to support the incompetents and the ne'er do-wells, and the will-nots, and it is time we stopped it.[9]

Rockefeller Should Pay Same Tax Rate as You

Mr. Fuller: . . . According to your statement here you criticize the proposed graduated schedule of taxation. Are you in favor of that kind of a tax? . . .

Mr. Chandler: I probably would tax all incomes on the same basis. . . .

Mr. Fuller: In other words, you think that Mellon and Morgan and Ford, who make millions of dollars a year net profit, ought to be taxed on an equality with the little fellow who makes $500 or $1,000 or $10,000 a year net?

• • •

Mr. Chandler: Well, you are taking an extreme case which sounds bad and would look bad in the record.

Mr. Fuller: Well, will you answer the question?

Mr. Chandler: I think that as an abstract proposition of justice, taxation should be equal upon all classes. But when you talk about these huge fortunes, about incomes of men like Rockefeller and Mellon—those men immediately reinvest their money in productive enterprise and use it for the employment of labor, and they make two blades of grass grow where one grew before.[10]

Congress Considers: 2. Economic Effect

The certainty of reward for effort, mental and physical, is the reason why the people of this country have built up a wealth. . . .

Take away that reward and the effort stops; the source then dries up.[11]

—George Marklan, president of Philadelphia Board of Trade

The assumption that the owners of . . . capital would prefer no income at all to an income from which the government took half or even more, does not deserve fearful or prayerful consideration.[12]

—The Reverend John A. Ryan

. . . This amazing philosophy of redistribution of wealth through taxation. . . . is the aspect of this bill which has aroused the greatest indignation among businessman and private investors. It destroys confidence and is the arch foe of recovery.[13]

—George B. Chandler, Secretary of Ohio Chamber of Commerce

Anything that will decrease the consumptive capacity will not improve the stability of the productive investment.[14]

—Joseph D. McGoldrick, Joint Committee on Unemployment

Marklan Wants to Encourage Industry

Mr. Marklan: We are living in the greatest age of our history. There are more things more widely distributed in the hands of more people than ever before or than anywhere else in the world. We should now be building monuments to men like Carnegie, Rockefeller, Edison, Mellon, Ford . . . and a thousand and one others like them who have created and distributed more wealth to more people than all the professors, socialists, communists, and their ilk ever dreamed of. . . .

The dollar circulates only through industry, and industry is a delicate mechanism not to be tampered with. Industry creates all the wealth and distributes it. I suggest that you study industry and its needs rather than how you can milk it and blame it for everything under the sun. The banker, lawyer, bond and stock broker, department store, chain store, retail store, and realtor all thrive when the wheels of industry turn.

So, let us study how to keep them turning. . . . Extravagant government and consequent high taxes will not do it. We might get along with less taxes; perhaps that would help and perhaps it would do it. . . .

Mr. Cooper: How much thought have you given to the wild and foolish statements you have made?

Mr. Marklan: Have I made any?

Mr. Cooper: All of them.

Mr. Marklan: Do you work for a living? Are you in business?

The Chairman: The time of the gentlemen has expired. The next witness is . . .[15]

Underconsumptionists Would Tax Savers

Mr. McGoldrick: It is generally agreed, for example, however, that we are suffering from overproduction. Overproduction, however, is purely relative, whereas the corollary is underconsumption. Underconsumption has made many an otherwise sound investment unsafe. . . .

We, therefore, urge that the committee consider seriously the restoration of surtaxes which was unappropriately abandoned, and the imposition of substantial estate taxes. . . .

Mr. Rainey: May I ask the doctor one or two questions on underconsumption? How are you going to make people consume more wheat?

Mr. McGoldrick: The fact of the matter is that people with incomes of less than $10,000, in my opinion, spend practically all of their incomes. Take away one-half million dollars in taxes from that, and they would have that much less to spend. As for getting them to spend that on one thing and another thing, that is what advertisers are busily engaged in trying to do.

Mr. Rainey: Could we advertise sufficiently to make people use all the . . . wheat that we can produce, and we produce 200,000,000 bushels per year more than we consume?

Mr. McGoldrick: No; overproduction of that sort is probably impossible to absorb. On the other hand, if the incomes were substantially increased, then we could absorb a very great deal of your . . . wheat. . . .

Mr. Rainey: In other words, your position is that as to the small incomes, we ought to preserve them as much as we can and increase them as much as we can, and cut down the big incomes and the big estates as much as we can, and make them contribute to this fund to carry on the government?

Mr. McGoldrick: Yes; . . . at the present time we have two alternatives, that of taxing the capital income—that is, incomes above $10,000, which largely look for investment opportunity or speculative opportunities—or of taxing the wage earners and the middle classes. If you tax the latter, they have just that much less with which to buy. . . .[16]

Industry Needs Reassurance

Mr. Seidman: . . . I think the reassurance of industry would put more capital into operation and into production and into employment than the government can ever hope to do, by spending government money. . . .

Mr. Lewis: What do you mean sir; by reassuring industry? Hoover's administration, I think, gave them everything they wanted, did they get any reassurance?

Mr. Seidman: . . . My own feeling about the reassurance of industry is this. Industry does not know whether if it invests capital it will be taxed out of existence first, or whether the policy and the method of the government will so change as to make a man feel that he might just as well put his money in a bank, or a vault, or tax-exempt securities than risk it where he does not know how much of it will disappear. . . .

Mr. Lewis: . . . Do you know anything specific that the administration or the government can do that will reassure business?

Mr. Seidman: . . . The most desirable thing the government can do today is to state to the nation that we realize that we have been spending beyond our present means.

Mr. Lewis: Do you mean that capital has gone on strike against improvements in industry because of the relief rolls?

Mr. Seidman: . . . Probably it is only human nature for a man to try to conserve his capital and risk it only when he knows he can make a profit.

The Chairman: Is there anything that the government ought to have done, or can do, to assure industry with certainty that it will make a profit? That is the most astounding statement I have ever heard a witness make.

Mr. Seidman: No; but I think the government can assure industry that it will not do things which will result in loss to industry.

The Chairman: . . . Would you allow industry to be its own doctor and write a prescription before the government should do anything? . . .[17]

Production More Important Than Consumption, Says Mills

Secretary Mills [Hoover's Secretary of the Treasury]: I am not interested, here, in the individual point of view. Taking the large point of view and looking at the life of a nation, what consequence is it whether for a short term of 25 or 30 years a particular individual or 10 or 20 individuals do control a certain amount of capital. What does that mean in the life of the nation? Nothing, if those funds during those years are all being productively used to increase the wealth of the nation through increased industrial capacity and the production of goods and the satisfaction of human wants.

Senator Couzens: The point arises, though, Mr. Secretary, as to how that is distributed while that earning power is going on.

Secretary Mills: I do not think that that is the real point, Senator Couzens.

Senator Couzens: Well, I know you do not, but I do.[18]

Congress Considers: 3. Raise Revenues

We have pointed out that by applying the British rate of taxation to high incomes in the United States we would have, in 1928, been able to secure total revenue of five and three-quarter billions as against a little over one billion dollars which we did secure through the tax on incomes in 1928. In other words, about five times as much revenue would have been secured as was secured.

Also in 1932, the revenue would have been $1,128,000,000 as against $324,-000,000 now raised through that kind of a tax.

When you compare the rate of taxation in the United States and in Great Britain, we find that on incomes of between fifty and one hundred thousand dollars per year in the United States the tax is 17 percent, whereas the tax in Britain is 39 percent.[19]
—Herbert Benjamin, New York City.

A basic principle underlying individual income taxation is that high rates do not in themselves produce large revenues.

. . . The 1928 Revenue Act was the most moderate since the war. The maximum surtax income tax rate was 20 percent. . . . In that year the personal income tax yielded the highest amount in peace-time history—$1,164,000,000. In 1932 the income tax yielded but $328,000,000, a shrinkage of almost three-fourths. In other words, that is a shrinkage in those two years of several times more than what is supposed to be raised by higher rates included in the House bill. Since there had been no alteration in rates in the years mentioned, these figures indicate the small effect which rates have on revenues as contrasted with the base of such taxes.[20]
—Fred Clausen, U.S. Chamber of Commerce.

Congress Decides

The tax rates Congress approved in 1935 are listed at left, along with the rates in effect during selective years between 1936 and 1965. The effect of these rates on actual distribution of income is shown on the next chart. These rates had only a minimal effect on distribution of income because loopholes in the law allowed the very wealthy to escape taxation, and because most taxes (especially state and local) took a disproportionately larger amount from low income groups; they were regressive rather than progressive.

For a complete description of the total taxation on various income classes, see the last chart. On the basis of all the evidence decide what changes should be made in our tax structure—that is, who should pay and how much?

Regressive and Progressive Taxes

A tax is considered "progressive" if the rate (not the total amount) of taxation increases as income increases. A "regressive" tax is one that reduces the rates as income mounts.

State sales taxes fall proportionately more on the poor than the rich because the poor spend a larger percentage of their incomes. This is true for taxes on standard equipment such as washing machines and cars, as well as on cosmetics, cigarettes, and liquor. Property taxes, like sales taxes, tend to hurt the less well-to-do because a much larger percentage of income is tied up in property. Social Security taxes (see Chapter 14) fall most heavily on the poor since the tax is based only on the first $6600 dollars of income. Therefore, all the taxes mentioned above tend to be regressive, for the tax rate decreases as income increases.

The only truly progressive tax is an income tax, in which the rate of taxation increases with income. But even under income taxes, wealthier

FEDERAL INCOME TAX RATES, 1936-65[a]

Taxable income ($000)[b]	1936-39[c]	1944-45	1946-47[d]	1948-49[d]	1952-53	1954-63	1964	1965
Under 0.5	4	23	19.0	16.6	22.2	20	16.0	14
0.5- 1.0							16.5	15
1.0- 1.5							17.5	16
1.5- 2.0							18.0	17
2.0- 4.0	4	25	20.9	19.4	24.6	22	20.0	19
4.0- 6.0	8	29	24.7	22.9	29.0	26	23.5	22
6.0- 8.0	9	33	28.5	26.4	34.0	30	27.0	25
8.0- 10.0	10	37	32.3	29.9	38.0	34	30.5	28
10.0- 12.0	11	41	36.1	33.4	42.0	38	34.0	32
12.0- 14.0	12	46	40.8	37.8	48.0	43	37.5	36
14.0- 16.0	13	50	44.6	41.4	53.0	47	41.0	39
16.0- 18.0	15	53	47.5	44.0	56.0	50	44.5	42
18.0- 20.0	17	56	50.4	46.6	59.0	53	47.5	45
20.0- 22.0	19	59	53.2	49.3	62.0	56	50.5	48
22.0- 26.0	21	62	56.0	51.9	66.0	59	53.5	50
26.0- 32.0	23	65	58.9	54.6	67.0	62	56.0	53
32.0- 38.0	25	68	61.8	57.2	68.0	65	58.5	55
38.0- 44.0	28	72	65.6	60.7	72.0	69	61.0	58
44.0- 50.0	31	75	68.4	63.4	75.0	72	63.5	60
50.0- 56.0	35 }	78	71.2	66.0	77.0	75	66.0	62
56.0- 60.0	39 }							
60.0- 62.0	39 }	81	74.1	68.6	80.0	78	68.5	64
62.0- 68.0	43 }							
68.0- 70.0	47 }							
70.0- 74.0	47 }	84	77.0	71.3	83.0	81	71.0	66
74.0- 80.0	51 }							
80.0- 90.0	55	87	79.8	73.9	85.0	84	73.5	68
90.0-100.0	59	90	82.6	76.6	88.0	87	75.0	69
100.0-136.7 }	62	92	84.6	78.3 }	90.0	89	76.5	70
136.7-150.0 }				80.3 }				
150.0-200.0	64	93	85.5	81.2	91.0	90	76.5	70
over 200.0[e]	f	94	86.4	82.1	92.0	91	77.0	70

[a] Compiled from U.S. Treasury Department, *Statistics of Income,* annual volumes; *The Federal Revenue System: Facts and Problems, 1961,* Joint Economic Committee, 87th Congress, 1st Session (1961), p. 208; and Revenue Act of 1964 (P.L. 88-272). Rates apply to calendar years shown. Rates for 1940-43 and 1950-51 were between those for adjacent periods.

[b] Surtax net income prior to 1954. For 1948 and later years, the rate brackets for husbands and wives filing joint returns are twice as wide as those shown, which apply to single persons and separate returns of husbands and wives. For 1952 and later years, separate schedules are applied to unmarried heads of households, providing approximately one-half the benefits of income splitting by husbands and wives.

individuals frequently find loopholes that permit them to escape the steep higher rates of taxation. That is why the rich may often pay proportionately lower taxes than the poor.

Who Does Pay?

The percentage of a family's income paid in taxes (federal, state, and local) is often higher for poor families than it is for wealthy families. A recent survey showed that families with incomes under $2,000 paid more than 38 percent of their earnings in taxes in 1960, while families earning between $7,500 and $10,000 paid only 22.3 percent. By 1966, because of several federal tax cuts and rises in local taxes, the poor paid even a larger percentage of the total taxes than they did in 1960. Under the 1964 tax cut as first proposed, a family of four earning $1 million a year, using the loopholes allowed by the law, would pay on the average a total federal tax of only 24 percent; in 1939 the situation was not much different.

EFFECT OF THE AMERICAN TAX SYSTEM ON THE VARIOUS INCOME CLASSES

Income class range	Mean income	Percentage of all income units	Percentage of income paid out in taxes		
			Federal	State and local	Total
Under $500	$ 346	17.0	7.9	14.0	21.9
$500–$1000	847	29.5	6.6	11.4	18.0
$1000–$1500	1,381	22.1	6.4	10.9	17.3
$1500–$2000	1,929	13.1	6.6	11.2	17.8
$2000–$3000	2,689	11.3	6.4	11.1	17.5
$3000–$5000	4,121	4.6	7.0	10.6	17.6
$5000–$10,000	7,741	1.5	8.4	9.5	17.9
$10,000–$15,000	12,872	.4	14.9	10.6	25.5
$15,000–$20,000	19,477	.2	19.8	11.9	31.7
$20,000 and over	47,600	.3	27.2	10.6	37.8
Total	$ 1,693	100.0	9.2	11.0	20.2

Source: Sidney Ratner, *Taxation and Democracy in America,* (New York: John Wiley and Sons, Inc., 1967), 2nd ed., p. 513.

---

[c]Does not reflect earned income credit, which reduced rates shown by a maximum of 0.4 percentage points up to a net income of $14,000.

[d]After reductions from tentative tax.

[e]Subject to maximum effective rate limitations as follows: 1944–45, 90 percent; 1946–47, 85.5 percent; 1948–49, 77 percent; 1952–53, 88 percent; 1954–63, 87 percent.

[f]Range of 66 percent to a maximum of 79 percent on surtax net income in excess of $5 million.

Source: Richard Goode, *The Individual Income Tax* (Washington: The Brookings Institution, 1964), p. 324.

PERCENTAGE OF NATIONAL PERSONAL INCOME RECEIVED BY EACH INCOME-
TENTH AFTER FEDERAL INCOME TAXES

	Highest	2nd	3rd	4th	5th	6th	7th	8th	9th	Lowest
1947	31(−2)*	15	12	10	9	8(+1)	6	5(+1)	3	1
1949	28(−2)	15	13(+1)	11	9	8	7(+1)	5	3	1
1950	27(−2)	15	13	11	10(+1)	8	7(+1)	5	3	1
1951	28(−3)	15	13(+1)	11(+1)	9	8	7(+1)	5	3	1
1952	27(−3)	15	13(+1)	11	10(+1)	8	7(+1)	5	3	1
1953	28(−3)	15	12	11(+1)	9	8	7(+1)	5	4(+1)	1
1954	27(−2)	15	13	11	9	8	7(+1)	5	4(+1)	1
1955	27(−2)	16	13	11	10(+1)	8	6	5(+1)	3	1

*Numbers in parentheses indicate change in percentage points from before-tax income.

Compiled from Bureau of the Census, *Statistical Abstract of the United States, 1957* (Washington, D.C.: U.S. Government Printing Office, 1957), p. 309. These data, collected by the Survey Research Center, include capital gains but exclude income-in-kind.

Source: Gabriel Kolko, *Wealth and Power in America,* (New York: Frederick A. Praeger, 1962) p. 34.

NOTES

1. Franklin D. Roosevelt, *The Public Papers and Addresses of Franklin D. Roosevelt,* ed. Samuel I. Rosenman, vol IV (New York: Random House, 1938), pp. 272–274.

2. "Topics of the Day," *The Literary Digest,* July 6, 1935, p. 4.

3. United States Congress, House of Representatives, Committee on Ways and Means, *Proposed Taxation of Individual and Corporate Incomes, Inheritance and Gifts,* hearings, 74th Congress, 1st Session, July 8–13, 1935 (Washington, D.C.: U.S. Government Printing Office, 1935), p. 168.

4. *Ibid.,* p. 318.

5. *Ibid.,* pp. 56, 60.

6. *Ibid.,* p. 128.

7. *Ibid.,* p. 173.

8. United States Congress, Senate, Committee on Appropriations, *Emergency Relief Appropriations Act, Fiscal Year 1943,* 77th Congress, 2nd Session, on H. J. R. 324 (Washington, D.C.: U.S. Government Printing Office, 1943), p. 895.

9. *Proposed Taxation of Individual and Corporate Incomes,* etc. p. 128.

10. *Ibid.,* p. 181.

11. *Ibid.,* p. 128.

12. United States Congress, Senate, Committee on Finance, *Revenue Act of 1932,* 72nd Congress, 1st Session, on H.R. 19236, April 6–21, 1932 (Washington, D.C.: U.S. Government Printing Office, 1932), p. 144.

13. *Proposed Taxation of Individual and Corporate Incomes,* etc., p. 172.

14. United States Congress, House of Representatives, Committee on Ways and Means, *Revenue Revision, 1932,* 72nd Congress, 1st Session, January 13–17 and February 2, 4, 1932 (Washington, D.C.: U.S. Government Printing Office, 1932), p. 191.

15. *Proposed Taxation of Individual and Corporate Incomes,* etc., pp. 128–130.

16. *Revenue Revision, 1932,* pp. 191, 194–195.

17. *Proposed Taxation of Individual and Corporate Incomes,* etc., pp. 72–73.
18. *Revenue Act of 1932,* pp. 39–40.
19. *Proposed Taxation of Individual and Corporate Incomes,* etc., p. 325.
20. United States Congress, Senate, Committee on Finance, *Revenue Act of 1935,* 74th Congress, 1st Session, on H.R. 8974, July 30–August 8, 1935 (Washington, D.C.: U.S. Government Printing Office, 1935), p. 257.

QUESTIONS

1. Should federal tax policies aim at reducing differences in incomes? Explain with specific reference to income distribution in any given year.
2. Do high taxes discourage business investments? Do low taxes on the rich encourage too much saving?
3. Do you think the tax burden today falls too heavily on the poor?

SUGGESTED READING

Simon Kuznets, *Shares of Upper Groups in Income and Savings* (New York: National Bureau of Economic Research, 1950) is technical, but a classic study of income distribution in the United States. Kuznets argues that wealth is unequally distributed in this country. Randolph E. Paul, *Taxation in the United States* (Boston: Little, Brown and Company, 1954) is the standard history on the subject. Daniel Casey and William Helm use historical examples and emotional arguments to present a case against progressive income taxes and for tax reduction in *Slash Those Taxes* (New York: Dwell, Sloan, and Pearce, 1948). Gabriel Kolko in *Wealth and Power in America* (New York: Frederick A. Praeger, 1962) proves the poor actually pay a larger share of their income in taxes than the rich. Herman Miller in *Rich Man, Poor Man* (New York: Thomas Y. Crowell, 1964) uses diagrams to explain the maldistribution of income in the United States.

Chapter 17
President Roosevelt
and the Supreme Court

Introduction

When the Federal Constitution was written in 1787, America consisted of thirteen semi-independent states strung along the Atlantic seaboard. At that time 90 percent of its population were farmers and the sea was the major artery of communication between the states. It is unlikely that any of the fifty-five men who wrote the Constitution could have imagined that the original thirteen states would expand into fifty, stretched across a mighty continent, linked by steel rails, pipelines, telephone wires, radios, and airplanes. But as the country grew the powers of its government expanded.

With few important exceptions, the process of adapting the Constitution to the twentieth century occurred without amending it. Instead, the Supreme Court gradually interpreted the articles of the Constitution in light of the needs of the times. Thus, the power to regulate "commerce among the states" once meant preventing states from obstructing trade among themselves, but in the 1870's it came to mean preventing railroads from overcharging customers for hauling goods across state lines. In the early 1900's, the commerce clause meant granting Congress power to prevent interstate shipments of foods or drugs that endangered people's health. Did it also mean Congress could prevent shipment of goods made by children under sixteen years of age or by underpaid women workers? Woodrow Wilson and his Congress said yes, but the Court said no.

Did Congress have the power to regulate manufacturing, to prescribe workers' hours, minimum wages, and working conditions? During the 1930's, President Roosevelt and Congress formulated the New Deal answer to these questions: Yes, the Constitution's commerce clause gave the government the right to regulate manufacturing, and mining and agriculture as well. But the justices on the Supreme Court clung to the opposite answer: No, the commerce clause was meant to be interpreted strictly, and manufacturing, mining, and farming were local activities, outside of congressional control. Consequently, much important New Deal legislation, including the Agricultural Adjustment Act and the National Recovery Administration, was declared unconstitutional.

Normally, a president does not have power to modify the Supreme Court's opinions unless he has the good fortune of choosing replacements for retiring justices. Roosevelt feared the Court would invalidate his entire New Deal program before he could appoint new judges. He therefore proposed that Congress give him the power to appoint additional justices to "assist" those over the age of 70, unless the older men retired voluntarily. But this approach raised at least as many questions as it answered. If the president (and Congress) could change the Court to conform with their ideas, what was the purpose of having a Court?

This chapter tells of the conflict between Roosevelt and the Court and shows how it was resolved. But the reader must bear in mind that the issue of judicial review of laws is a timeless question, and that there is no pat method of assuring a flexible constitution that also imposes restraints on the will of the majority in order to protect the rights of the minority.

The Court Decides on the Schecter "Blue Eagle" Case

The time was high noon; the date, Monday, May 27, 1935; the place, the dignified old building that once housed the United States Senate and was now used by the Supreme Court to announce its decisions. Almost 300 people packed the small, semicircular chamber. Enveloped in their somber black robes, the nine justices of the Supreme Court sat behind the bench facing their hushed audience. Bearded and solemn, Chief Justice Charles Evans Hughes in his high-backed chair was flanked by associate justices, who were formally arranged on either side of him according to years of service with the Court.

All attention was focused on the strong face of the Chief Justice as he read his decision in the case, *Schecter v. the United States.* Hughes' silver hair glistened in the sunlight streaming through the latticed skylight on the ceiling. His words echoed across the silent room. The Court had decided against the government. The Live Poultry Code, embodying regulations by the National Recovery Administration, was unconstitutional.

The Schecters bought poultry shipped from outside New York State. But Justice Hughes claimed the poultry could not be considered in interstate commerce because: ". . . the poultry was trucked to their [the Schecters'] slaughterhouses in Brooklyn for local disposition and sale. The interstate transactions in relationship to that poultry then ended."[1]

Therefore, Hughes concluded, the poultry industry is a local business, subject to state power, but not to federal regulation. The National Recovery Administration, by regulating wages, hours, and business practices in New York's poultry markets, was acting unconstitutionally. The law, granting Congress that power, the National Industrial Recovery Act, was unconstitutional because it had mistakenly assumed that the national government had power over production.

As Justice Hughes announced the Court's decision, NRA head Donald Richburg turned ashen white, but said nothing.

A Return to "Horse and Buggy" Days

Four days later, President Roosevelt unburdened himself to the press. The Court's decision, he told a news conference, was the most important since the Dred Scott case, for ". . . We have been relegated to the horse and buggy definition of interstate commerce. . . ."[2]

Roosevelt felt that the NRA decision distorted the true meaning of the commerce power. The President wondered:

> Does this decision mean that the United States government has no control over any national economic problem?
>
> The simple example is crop adjustment. Are we going to take the hands of the federal government completely off any effort to adjust the growing of national crops, and go right straight back to the old principle that every farmer is a lord of his own farm and can do anything he wants, raise anything any old time, in any quantity and sell any time he wants? You and I know perfectly well that if we completely abandon crop control . . . we shall again have 36 cent wheat. You can't stop it. Under present world conditions we will have 5 cent cotton. That is obvious. . . .[3]

The Agricultural Adjustment Act Declared Unconstitutional

The judges' reply to the President was not long in coming. In 1936, the Supreme Court scrapped the Agricultural Adjustment Act; like the National Industrial Recovery Act it was held unconstitutional. Justice Roberts this time wrote the majority opinion in a drastic judicial attack upon the President's farm program:

> Its stated purpose is the control of agricultural production, a purely local activity, in an effort to raise the prices paid the farmer. Indeed, . . . the commerce clause, . . . for the purpose of the present case, may be put aside as irrelevant. . . .[4]

Court Holds Mining and Manufacturing Outside Congressional Reach

In the same year, the Supreme Court set aside as unconstitutional another major item of New Deal legislation. A narrow definition of the commerce clause, declaring that production was a purely local activity and not subject to federal regulation, again played a central part. In ruling on the Guffey Bituminous Coal Act of 1935, Justice Sutherland spoke for the Court. He declared that the regulation of wages and prices in the coal industry was unconstitutional because the interstate commerce clause did not grant Congress the power to regulate manufacturing: ". . . the local character of mining, of manufacturing and of crop growing is a fact, and remains a fact, whatever may be done with the products. . . ."[5]

The Guffey decision again made Roosevelt feel that the Court was depriving Congress of the right to legislate on national economic problems.

After all, 97 percent of the coal produced by the company Sutherland had just ruled out of interstate commerce was sold outside the state in which it was mined.

Criticism of the Court

By rigidly defining interstate commerce to mean only goods actually moving between states, the Supreme Court claimed to be protecting the rights of states against the powers of the national government. But in a split decision in 1936, the Court declared unconstitutional a New York State law setting a minimum wage for women, thus also denying states the right to protect their citizens (a decision in Harding's era had already invalidated federal minimum wages). Decisions of this kind prompted John L. Lewis, head of the United Mine Workers Union, to exclaim: "It is a sad commentary on our form of government when every decision of the Supreme Court seems designed to fatten capital and to starve and destroy labor."[6]

There were others who complained that the economic philosophy of the justices and not the compulsions of the language of the Constitution were the cause of the Court's disagreement with constitutional interpretations. Even a restless minority among the Supreme Court justices wondered how far the Court should go in invalidating laws which successive popularly elected congressional majorities believed to be constitutional. Dissenting in the Guffey case on regulation of coal mines, Justice Cardozo said the Constitution did not condemn Congress "to inactivity in the face of price wars and wage wars. . . . The Fifth Amendment does not include the right to persist in this anarchic riot."[7]

Dissenting in the AAA case, Justice Stone said, "The only check upon our own exercise of power is our own sense of self-restraint." Opposing the Court's invalidation of agricultural controls and processing taxes, Stone declared that "the power to tax and spend includes the power to relieve a nationwide economic maladjustment."[8]

Hughes, Brandeis, Cardozo, and Stone dissented in the minimum wage case. Stone was unusually frank, saying in his dissent that he could find no basis for the majority's decision "other than our own personal economic predilections." He jabbed at the Court's laissez-faire ideas of workers' contracts: "There is grim irony in speaking of the freedom of contract of those who, because of their economic necessities, give their services for less than is needful to keep body and soul together."[9]

The Constitution and the Elections of 1936

When Supreme Court interpretations become an issue between the parties, the people have a voice in the next elections. On June 2, 1936, just after the Court's decision against minimum wage laws, Roosevelt said that the Court was reading into the Constitution a "'no-man's land' where no government—state or federal—can function. . . . A state cannot do it, and the federal government cannot do it."[10]

It happened over there — it can happen here.

The example of Hitler and Mussolini led some Americans to fear that
an unchecked Roosevelt would stop at nothing.

On June 27, Roosevelt was renominated. In the keynote speech, Senator
Barkley flayed "smug and cynical apostles" of laissez-faire who cheered
Supreme Court interpretations. "Is the Court beyond criticism?" asked
Barkley, and he quoted Abraham Lincoln to the contrary. Today, declared
Barkley, "The judges have decided that, under the Constitution, the fed-
eral government cannot lift men, women, and children out of the degrada-
tion of unconscionable hours, wages, or working conditions . . . because
it invades the rights of property."[11]

Roosevelt's campaign speeches did not make conservative justices an
open target, but the party platform said that if the needed laws were not
adjudged to be "within the Constitution, we shall seek such clarifying
amendment as will assure . . . the several states and the Congress . . . the
power to enact those laws."[12]

Republican campaigners harped on "independence of the judiciary"
and echoed ex-President Hoover's remark, "Thank God for the Supreme
Court!" Hoover himself in a campaign speech flatly asked Roosevelt

Just a minute.

Opposition to court-packing — obstructionism or statesmanship?

whether he planned to "stuff" the Supreme Court. Roosevelt, in his final speech, listed specific proposed enactments which he asked voters to endorse with an election mandate: the list included the Wagner Act and Social Security Act (both already held unconstitutional by lower courts) and it also included minimum wage laws and the coal and agricultural enactments which the Supreme Court had overthrown. Roosevelt won an overwhelming victory at the polls that fall.

The President's "Court Packing" Plan

A message from Roosevelt to Congress on February 5, 1937, burst like a bombshell. His proposed Judiciary Reorganization bill stressed greater court efficiency, speeding up the decisions on cases, and the need of additional judges—"younger blood will vitalize the courts." He would add a justice to the Supreme Court for each justice who was over seventy and pension off judges over seventy who were willing to retire. On March 9, he defended his plan:

Since the rise of the modern movement for social and economic progress through legislation, the Court has more and more often and more boldly asserted a power to veto laws passed by the Congress and State legislatures. . . .

In the last four years the sound rule of giving statutes the benefit of all reasonable doubt has been cast aside. . . .

This plan will save our National Constitution from hardening of the judicial arteries. . . .[13]

Opposition to Court Packing

The Senate Judiciary Committee considered Roosevelt's proposals and emphatically disagreed with him. The Committee's report asserted that the framers of the Constitution separated the power of President, Congress, and Supreme Court so no one man or group could dominate. Who would be left to protect the Constitution if the President could dispose of a Court that limited his powers? In fiery language the Committee advised that Roosevelt's "court packing" scheme be rejected:

We know that this instrument [the Constitution] . . . was carefully planned and deliberately framed to establish three coordinate branches of government, every one of them to be independent of the others. For the protection of the people, for the preservation of the rights of the individual, for the maintenance of the liberties of minorities, for maintaining the checks and balances of our dual system, the three branches of the government were so constituted that the independent expression of honest difference of opinion could never be restrained in the people's servants and no one branch could overawe or subjugate the others. That is the American system. It is immeasurably more important, immeasurably more sacred to the people of America, indeed, to the people of all the world than the immediate adaptation of any legislation however beneficial. . . .[14]

The Senatorial Committee saw the issue as unwarranted interference with the Supreme Court, which, if permitted, would mean the Court would cease to be independent of either Congress or the President, and unable to check their power. The President saw the issue as judicial supremacy over Congress, which would thwart the will of the people as expressed by their elected representatives.

"A Switch in Time"

Even before President Roosevelt delivered his "court packing" message, changes occurred within the Supreme Court itself which seemed to decrease the need for reorganization. In a notable decision of 1937 on the Wagner Act, a law to insure collective bargaining, the Court surprised many by reversing the limitations on Congress's power over interstate commerce that it had proclaimed in the Guffey decision.* Compare the following words from Justice Hughes' decision in the Wagner Act case with the opinion in the Guffey Act of 1935 on page 145.

---

*The opinion was written but not delivered before Roosevelt asked to reorganize the Court.

The fundamental principle is that the power to regulate commerce is the power to enact "all appropriate legislation" for "its protection and advancement . . ."; to adopt measures "to promote its growth and insure its safety . . ."; "to foster, protect, control and restrain. . . ." That power may be exerted to protect interstate commerce "no matter what the source of the dangers which threaten it."

Although activities may be *intrastate* in character when separately considered, if they have such a close and substantial relation to interstate commerce that their control is essential or appropriate to protect that commerce from burdens and obstructions, Congress cannot be denied the power to exercise that control. . . .[15]

What caused this switch? It is hard to say. Perhaps the Court sensed popular resentment to its decisions and therefore began conforming more closely with public opinion. Perhaps the case was sufficiently different to warrant a reversal of the Guffey Act opinion. But, for whatever reason, the Court came very close to Roosevelt's understanding of the commerce clause. This broad interpretation of constitutional power was also exhibited in an opinion upholding the Social Security Act. In 1937, the Court again reversed itself and held a minimum wage law constitutional, though a few months prior it invalidated a New York law to the same effect. In May, 1937, Justice Van Devanter announced his impending retirement, at last giving Roosevelt an opportunity to appoint a new justice.*

The Court's shift to a broad interpretation of the commerce clause made "court packing" seem unnecessary and helped defeat Roosevelt's attempt to enlarge the Court. "A switch in time that saved nine," one reporter suggested. And the American people were spared the agony of deciding between the Court and the legislation they desired.

Indeed, Roosevelt lost the battle to enlarge the Court, but won the war over a broader interpretation of the commerce clause. Today the Supreme Court freely recognizes congressional authority over a wide spectrum of activities ranging from agriculture to minimum wages and civil rights. Attacks on the Court now come from opponents of extension of Congress's power, rather than from those who, like Roosevelt, favor its extension.

---

*Eventually Roosevelt was able to appoint six new justices to the Supreme Court, which entirely changed its composition and placed it squarely behind the Roosevelt interpretation of the commerce clause.

NOTES

1. Franklin D. Roosevelt, *The Public Papers and Addresses of Franklin D. Roosevelt,* ed. Samuel I. Rosenman, vol. IV (New York: Random House, 1938), p. 211.

2. *Ibid.,* p. 221.

3. *Ibid.,* pp. 212–213.

4. James Morton Smith and Paul L. Murphy, *Liberty and Justice—A Historical Record of American Constitutional Development* (New York: Alfred A. Knopf, 1958), p. 414.

5. *Ibid.,* p. 416.

6. Arthur M. Schlesinger, Jr., *The Politics of Upheaval* (Boston: Houghton Mifflin Company, 1960), p. 489.

7. 298 U.S. 587 (1936)

8. 297 U.S. 1 (1936)

9. 298 U.S. 587 (1936)

10. Roosevelt, *op. cit.,* pp. 191–192.

11. Charles and Mary Beard, *America in Midpassage* (New York: The Macmillan Company, 1939), p. 319.

12. *Current History,* XLIV (August, 1936), p. 52.

13. Ray A. Billington, Bert J. Loewenberg, and S. Hugh Brockunier, *The Making of American Democracy,* vol. II (New York: Holt, Rinehart and Company, Inc., 1957), pp. 446–447.

14. United States Congress, Senate Reports on Public Bills, *Reorganization of the Federal Judiciary,* Report No. 711, 75th Congress, 1st Session (Washington, D.C.: U.S. Government Printing Office, 1937), pp. 8–9, 14.

15. Smith and Murphy, *op. cit.,* p. 429.

QUESTIONS

1. Are manufacturing and mining local or national activities? Explain your answer and its implication on the power of the federal government.

2. Were changes in the Supreme Court necessary to fight the Depression? Explain.

3. Was American democracy endangered more by the Supreme Court's interpretation of the commerce clause than by the President's plan to enlarge the Court?

SUGGESTED READING

A study favorable to Roosevelt is Robert H. Jackson, *The Struggle for Judicial Supremacy* (New York: Alfred A. Knopf, 1941) and a disapproving account is given by Merlo J. Pusey, *The Supreme Court Crisis* (New York: The Macmillan Company, 1937). Charles Pritchett analyzes the judicial changes brought about by Roosevelt's appointees in *The Roosevelt Court, . . . 1937–1947* (New York: The Macmillan Company, 1948). For a compilation of conflicting views on court packing see A. H. Cope and Fred Krinskey (ed.), *Franklin D. Roosevelt and the Supreme Court* (Boston: D. C. Heath and Company, 1952, 1969). A first rate constitutional history, James Morton Smith and Paul L. Murphy, *Liberty and Justice — A Historical Record of American Constitutional Development* (New York: Alfred A. Knopf, 1958) helps the reader gain perspective on the issues involved in the fight for judicial supremacy.

UNIT IV.
ENDURING ECONOMIC PROBLEMS

The Great Depression ended in 1941, yet today one American out of six is still clutched in the vise of poverty; millions are still jobless (though the number has decreased significantly since 1963); 800 thousand farmers yearly leave their bankrupt farms often only to find unemployment in the cities, whose central sections decay as the slums grow and the well-to-do flee into the suburbs. These problems persist unsolved, even though many Americans enjoy the world's highest standard of living. Poverty amidst plenty is as much the dilemma for the 1970's as it was of the 1920's.

The focus of this unit is on modern poverty, the role of the government in the economy, and the problem of economic growth. Does the responsibility of the federal government extend to the eradication of poverty? Should the government incur deficits? Should it cut expenditures or raise taxes? How should it deal with the farm problem? The fate of the American economy hinges, among other things, on the reader's answers to these questions, for he will have a voice in deciding whether the 1970's and 1980's are to become "prosperity" or "depression" decades.

Chapter 18
The Farm Problem Today

Introduction

The farmers' depression during the 1920's was the forerunner of the far more widespread depression of the 1930's. If the country has learned from experience, it should be concerned about the continued prosperity of the farm population.

America's farmers have failed to obtain parity with the non-farm population in standards of living, despite a continuation of the agricultural programs initiated during the 1930's. Farm incomes remain far lower than factory incomes and farmers enjoy fewer luxuries than the people they clothe and feed. This failure is admitted and deplored by all who study the problem, but the experts are in sharp disagreement over proposed solutions. While some farm experts want gradually to phase all agricultural programs out of existence and return the farmer to the free market, others propose to raise farm income by direct income-subsidy payments. Meanwhile, among city dwellers there are taxpayers and consumers who are tired of paying farmers money only to see food prices steadily increase. But Congress cannot seem to find any other solution to the farm problem.

The farm problem has many faces. One is low farm income; another is the high cost of government programs for which the taxpayer is billed; a third is high food prices, due in part to the government program. This chapter sketches this multiphased problem and examines suggested solutions.

Low Farm Income

Willie Preston Canty is among the 43 percent of the nation's farmers (as of 1964) living on an income within the poverty line of less than $3 thousand a year. On April 13, 1964, Mr. Canty testified before the House Subcommittee on Labor. His story bears repeating for the light it sheds on the plight of the poor among America's farmers:

I am Willie Preston Canty. I live in Pinewood, Clarendon County, South Carolina. I have lived and worked on a farm all my life. I am still anxious to stay on a farm. I am now 56 years of age. I have a wife and three children to support. I have been operating a farm for 36 years. I raise four crops in addition to raising hogs and vegetables for my family as well as for sale.

Last year, I was able to raise 20 bales of cotton which grossed $3,000, $400 worth of tobacco with an allotment of one acre, and $100 for soybeans. I also raise some corn. My gross income from the farm was $3,500. After paying all expenses, I had about $1,200 left . . .

Many of my relatives and friends have left the farm because of heavy indebtedness and poor crop yield plus inability to get credit. I have found it very difficult to get proper credit from agencies which lend to other farmers. My friends who have gone to cities bring back some disturbing stories about the conditions in which they have to live in some areas. I should like to stay on my farm and raise my children in the country where I feel it is best for all of us; in fact, at my age, changing from the farm would not be easy or helpful.[1]

Cost of Government Programs

In Minnesota, a farmer made a profit of $8 thousand in one year merely by not planting corn. He rented a 300-acre farm and the government paid him 62.5 cents for every bushel of corn he might have but did not harvest. After October 1, and through the winter, he could graze his cows on the land. If he again left this plot idle the following summer, he could make another $8 thousand.

In Kansas, one farmer cashed the checks he received from the government farm program and banked $139,237. One group of farmers, totaling fewer than 100 thousand, were paid $1 billion by the government for participating in the farm program. The other more than 3 million farmers were paid $2 billion to hold foods and fibers off the market or to plant fewer acres. These programs helped raise the prices of agricultural commodities and cost the consumer $300 million in added food prices.

Causes of the Farm Problem

Many years ago someone predicted unlimited wealth for the man who could find a way to grow two blades of grass where one used to grow. With the help of agricultural experts, farmers have done much better than that. Yields per acre have risen over 70 percent since 1920, and today each farm worker harvests five times the food he gathered in the 1920's. In 1945, one farmer could produce enough food to feed 12 people; in 1965, he produced enough for 32 people. Did these phenomenal technical achievements make farmers wealthy? No. In 1964, 43 percent of all farm families lived in poverty; farm income, which had declined by 33 percent between 1945 and 1953, declined by another 11 percent between 1953 and 1964. Growing two blades of grass in the place of one apparently resulted in receiving one dollar in the place of two.

If farmers were to be blamed for causing the farm problem, the fault lay with their efficiency. Unlike businessmen, they were unable to tailor production to demand, and therefore continuously produced surpluses that depressed prices. Government programs were aimed at solving this problem, but they failed to do more than diminish it.

The Alternatives

The farm problem will probably not be solved under programs similar to those already tried. Should the government then stop helping farmers and permit lower prices to drive them off their farms? Should the government continue paying farmers not to plant while buying their surpluses, or should it embark on a new program of supplementing farm incomes with cash payments? Would any of these proposals solve the farm problem? An examination of the history of the farm program and some of the proposed solutions should help answer these questions.

The Farm Program in Later Years

World War II, more than Roosevelt's agricultural program during the 1930's, brought prosperity to the farm. The end of the war again jeopardized this prosperity. To prevent a collapse of agricultural prices similar to the collapse following World War I, Congress re-enacted an agricultural program of price supports and acreage reduction. By 1955, the Department of Agriculture was storing $9 billion worth of cotton, corn, wheat, and other products. The program cost taxpayers $5 billion each year.

When Dwight Eisenhower was elected president in 1952, he appointed Ezra Taft Benson as his Secretary of Agriculture. Benson did not believe in excessive help for farmers. In fact, he blamed the farm problem on the government's farm program:

> Government price and acreage control policies took away the initiative of management, making it impossible for farmers to make the most efficient use of their machinery. . . . Their principal result has been to pile up, in government bins, surpluses of farm products that have hung over the market like the sword of Damocles.[2]

Benson concluded that government price props led to continued surpluses. His reasoning went something like this: Artificially high prices encouraged farmers to get more production out of each acre because government checks were spent on fertilizers and machinery. Therefore, federal spending intended to induce the planting of fewer acres inevitably resulted in increasing yields per acre. In the meantime, Benson claimed, Americans tended to buy less meat and wheat because prices charged by butchers and bakers were too high. Foreigners bought fewer American farm products because government supports raised prices of American foods and fibers. Federal farm policy therefore encouraged overpricing and overproduction and discouraged sales.

Moreover, the federal farm program, it was alleged, was "habit-forming" and was sapping the traditionally independent farmer's freedom and vitality. This point of view was strongly expressed by Charles Shuman, head

**U.S. Availability of all Grain for Food Aid and
Food Aid Needs of 66 Developing Nations,
1970–1985**

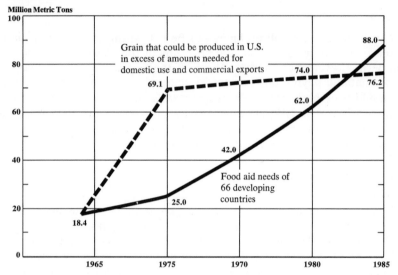

Million Metric Tons

Grain that could be produced in U.S.
in excess of amounts needed for
domestic use and commercial exports

88.0
74.0
69.1
76.2
62.0
42.0
Food aid needs of
66 developing
countries
25.0
18.4

1965   1975   1970   1980   1985

of the powerful American Farm Bureau Federation. When fully accustomed to the narcotic of government spending, Shuman claimed, the farmer would be helpless without his daily dose, for:

> Once in the habit, the victim becomes convinced he cannot live without the drug. In the jargon of the underworld—he is hooked. He'll do almost anything to get his next fix, his next check. The pushers, in this case the government bureaucrats and committees, constantly work to get more farmers hooked and dependent on payments.[3]

Shuman in effect was giving Benson's version of why agriculture is in trouble.

Benson's Farm Program

Secretary Benson directed his efforts to freeing American farmers from the drugging subsidy habit. He wanted gradually to reduce farm surpluses and price supports to get the farmers back to a free market basis. In 1954, Congress granted him permission to lower farm supports from 90 percent of parity to 82.5 percent, but it persistently refused to allow him still more leeway in reducing parity. Benson did his best to dispose of surpluses by enlarging markets for American farm produce and by establishing the Food for Peace program. This program gave several billion dollars of surplus foods to needy peoples throughout the world.

Benson evaluated the effects of his policies in three key commodities: hogs, dairy products, and beef.

The hog production and marketing situation has been sensibly adjusting. Our June report indicated that the 1956 spring pig crop was 8% below a year ago. This means that marketing should drop below last year's levels during summer and fall of 1956. We expect prices to reflect this reduced supply. Efficient producers who know their business will be free to plan hog production on their individual farms in keeping with sound management and good husbandry. No government planner will tell them how many sows they may breed, how heavy they should make their hogs, or when or where they must market them.[4]

In the dairy industry, Benson reported:

The burdensome surplus has been cut down, through unceasing efforts to find useful outlets. In July, 1954, the CCC butter inventory reached 467 million pounds. In mid-June of 1956 we had only 70,000 pounds of uncommitted supplies on hand. And for several weeks during March and April of 1956 our butter inventory was zero. We were "fresh out" and glad of it. Cheese has been our most difficult dairy surplus problem. But these stocks were cut 56 percent—from 436 million pounds in September 1954 to 193 million in June of 1956.[5]

And finally, Secretary Benson was able to report:

The American people literally ate us out of the worst of that beef problem. And that is a mighty good way of doing it. Consumers got added amounts of a fine, nutritious food. Above all, the beef problem was not made worse or made permanent by heavy stocks of beef, government-held or otherwise, hanging over future markets.[6]

Benson's methods for eliminating surpluses by "give-aways" under the Food for Peace program were continued by the Kennedy and Johnson administrations. It was reported in October, 1965, that the surplus of dairy products had disappeared, and after a sale of wheat to the Soviet Union the United States would have left just about enough for normal needs. As of August, 1966, only a few crops, chiefly cotton and tobacco, were still in oversupply. The Johnson administration wondered whether the time had come to encourage increases rather than decreases in production of some foods to fill domestic needs and to give more aid abroad by food shipments to peoples who suffered from continual hunger or outright starvation.

Evaluating Benson's Program

Agriculture Secretary Ezra Taft Benson was not chiefly concerned about foreign aid. He measured the success of his policies by reductions in farm surpluses and in surplus farmers in the United States. His programs did succeed in reducing surpluses and farmers. Between 1953 and 1964, one out of three farmers left his farm. In other respects, Benson was less successful. From 1953 to 1964, farm income declined by 11 percent while nonfarm income increased by 50 percent. Two out of five farmers continued to live in conditions officially classified as poverty; only 17 percent of the rest of the population was similarly distressed.

An evaluation of Benson's program requires a value judgment. Benson

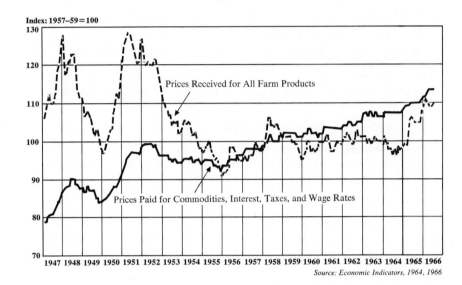

Index: 1957–59＝100

Source: *Economic Indicators, 1964, 1966*

was proud that his plan helped to reduce the number of people engaged in farming. But his critics were concerned as to whether farmers found jobs after arriving in the city, and the facts here are frightening: displaced farmers accounted for one-third of America's total unemployment in 1961. While Benson worried about farm surpluses piling up in government warehouses, his critics were concerned whether farm income was at par with non-farm income. And while Benson stressed overproduction, others noted that one-half of the world's population went hungry and one-fifth of America's population had a deficient diet.

The Farmer Held Responsible for a Shoddy Economy

During the 1950's, President Harry Truman's chief economic advisor was the amiable and stimulating Leon Keyserling. Since leaving the President's services in 1953, Keyserling headed the non-profit Conference on Economic Progress and criticized the economic policies of two Democratic and one Republican president. Keyserling, a devoted follower of Keynes, claimed that economic growth depends on demand, which the government must create when private industry cannot. Keyserling applied this principle to agriculture, where income had been declining steadily, and held the farm sector of the economy chiefly responsible for America's spotty economic performance during the 1950's and 1960's.

After the Korean War, or from 1953 until 1964, the American economy underwent a series of recessions that slowed down its rate of growth to approximately 3 percent. Had the economy used its resources efficiently and expanded at a 5 percent rate, Keyserling claimed, it would have produced another $590 billion worth of goods and services. Because these goods were not produced, each American family lost an average of $8750 over the eleven-year period. Keyserling traced between 20 to 25 percent of this loss to deficient farm income, which hurt industries selling to farmers. In other words, over a twelve-year period, the 11 percent decline in farm income led to a $120 billion reduction of national income. Keyserling's analysis gave added force to the words of his former boss, Harry Truman: "Prosperous farmers make for a prosperous nation and when farmers are in trouble, the nation is in trouble."

A New Farm Program

One possible solution to the farm problem is based on a proposal of G. E. Brandow. Although it has not received national publicity, important features have been enacted by Congress in 1963, 1964, and 1965. Judge this program on its merits and compare it to the Benson-Shuman proposals and to current programs.

In modified form, the Brandow plan emphasizes direct payments to individual farmers rather than acreage controls and crop loans. The farmer would be guaranteed an income based on his first 100 acres and 75 percent of the rest of his lands. Since he will not be compensated for the other 25 percent, he is encouraged but not forced to turn that land to other uses or to sell it. This will help reduce unprofitable use of the least productive acres. Meanwhile, food costs will decline somewhat because price supports are eliminated. Cheaper food prices will encourage higher domestic consumption and foreign sales.

In addition, direct income payments would be geared to help low-income farmers rather than wealthy agricultural businessmen. Rich farmers may receive a sliding scale of payments never in excess of $10 thousand. Poor farmers would be guaranteed an income substantially higher than they now receive.

The modified Brandow plan would operate something like this. A farmer harvesting 200 acres of cotton would keep all the proceeds earned from selling the cotton and receive a direct government payment for sales on all but 25 acres of his farm. These payments might equal ten cents for every pound of cotton he harvests. Not receiving any money for the last 25 acres would encourage him not to plant them. As the federal government would no longer keep prices at artificially high levels under this plan, consumers should benefit from low prices and buy more cotton goods. Direct government payment for every pound of cotton sold by farmers increases farm income and the farmer's purchasing power. This increased purchasing power benefits the economy.

The 1965 Farm Bill

In September, 1965, the *New York Times* reported on the Senate version of the 1965 farm bill. A bill with similar provisions had already been passed in the House, and President Johnson soon signed the final measure into law. The bill was to remain in effect for four years. The *New York Times* report on the bill is quoted below. Do the changes over previous farm bills represent an improvement? What features of the bill seem weak?

The bill continues the system of relatively low government support prices, supplemented by cash payments to the farmer for wheat, corn and other feed grains, and wool, and applies the principle for the first time to cotton, which is now the most troublesome and costly of the crops to which government programs apply.

Administration estimates are that the cotton change would save nearly $800 million over the next four crop years. . . .

On the whole, consumers would benefit by the bill, particularly in comparison with the former system of high price supports. For example, the low price of eggs and chicken in recent years has in part been a result of the lower corn prices that began with the drop in corn price supports. . . .

In a series of votes, the Senate consistently rejected today's proposals by Eastern Senators to impose varying dollar limits on the amount of government cash any one farmer could receive. The bill's managers successfully argued that such limits could break down the entire underlying system of supporting farm incomes and would hurt small farmers as much as large ones. . . .

At present, for example, if a large farmer places his entire crop of, say, rice in government hands, this amount is taken off the market and the price holds firm, giving a better return to the smaller growers.

The new system of cash payments with lower support and, hence, lower market prices, is designed to move nearly the entire crop into the market, both domestic and export. This has happened in the last two years for wheat and corn, though in the case of wheat foreign sales were greatly aided by virtual give-aways under the Food for Peace program. Government-held surpluses have declined.

In the case of cotton, the government support price would drop next year from the present 30 cents a pound to 21 cents, with probably even a lower price in subsequent years.

[In addition to the support price] farmers would get a cash payment of 9 cents a pound.[7]

Conclusion

This chapter has shown that the solutions of the 1930's failed to solve the farm problem after the war and down into the 1960's. Ezra Taft Benson and the American Farm Bureau Federation blamed the government for the farm problem and wanted gradually to end price supports; the modified Brandow plan would also end price supports but pay farmers directly to supplement their incomes on roughly 75 percent of their acreage, giving relatively more help to poor farmers while scaling down amounts paid to wealthy farmers. The 1965 farm program, which incorporates some of the provisions of the Brandow proposals, still maintains price supports and makes no special provisions for small farmers. The chapter asks the reader to decide whether the new farm bill moves in the right directions and whether any improvement should be recommended.

NOTES

1. United States Congress, House of Representatives, Committee on Education and Labor, *Economic Opportunity Act of 1964,* hearings before subcommittee on Poverty Program, 88th Congress, 2nd Session, on H.R. 10440, Part I, March 17–April 14, 1964 (Washington, D.C.: U.S. Government Printing Office, 1964), p. 539.
2. Ezra Taft Benson, *Farmers at the Crossroads* (New York: The Devin-Adair Company, 1956), p. 27.
3. "The Farm Fix," *Time,* December 18, 1964, p. 25.
4. Benson, *op. cit.,* p. 52.
5. *Ibid.,* p. 54.
6. *Ibid.,* p. 57.
7. *New York Times,* September 15, 1965, pp. 1, 27.

QUESTIONS

1. Which of the major aspects of the farm problem affects you directly? Indirectly?

2. Are there any compelling reasons why the U.S. government should not solve the farm problem by gradually phasing out all subsidies to farmers?

3. Which farm program, Brandow's, Benson's, or Roosevelt's, seemed preferable?

SUGGESTED READING

For a defense of the Eisenhower farm program see Ezra Taft Benson, *Cross Fire: The Eight Years with Eisenhower* (Garden City, N.Y.: Doubleday and Company, 1962), *Farmers at the Crossroads* (New York: The Devin-Adair Company, 1956), and *Freedom to Farm* (Garden City, N.Y.: Doubleday and Company, 1960). For the view that the decline in farm income was responsible for the general sluggish performance of the economy during the 1950's see Leon Keyserling, *Agriculture and the Public Interest* (Washington, D.C.: Conference on Economic Progress, 1965). On hunger in an age of production controls see Robert Cole, *Still Hungry in America* (New York: World Wide Publishing Company, 1969).

Chapter 19

Poverty U. S. A.

Introduction

America cherishes its reputation as a land of freedom and opportunity; a place where all have a chance to rise and few are poor. When President Hoover told his countrymen in 1929 that they stood at the threshold of an era when poverty would be abolished, he expressed an age-old dream. But, by the official definition of poverty,* one American in two was poor at the very moment the President spoke. The proportion of the poor dropped to one out of every six in the 1960's, and President Johnson launched a campaign to reduce it further; his was the first attempt in history to bring to all Americans the benefits of plenty. This chapter explores some of the issues raised by that attempt.

The Faces of Poverty: 1. Willie Johnson from Appalachia

Willie Johnson lives in a ten-state region commonly called Appalachia. Willie is 57 years old; he started working in the coal mines at age 13. Fourteen years ago he was earning $100 a week; now he earns nothing. Willie spends most of his day sitting on his sagging porch looking up at the mountain where a coal mine used to employ 500 men to produce 40 railroad cars of coal every day. The mine still produces 40 cars of coal, but the work is now done by 20 men.

In Logan county, where Willie lives, 14 thousand men were working in the mines in 1954; nine years later only 3500 were working and 10 thousand families were out of work. Most of them, like the Johnsons, live on relief. Willie has eight children, and his monthly welfare check is $165.

The Johnsons live in a four-room shack for which they pay $27 a month.

---

*The official definition of poverty is an income of $3,000 (at 1962 prices) or less for a family of four. This amount permits spending 70 cents for food per person per day. Allotments for clothes, rent, etc., are equally small.

The ten people in the house share four beds. The roof leaks and there is no running water. To save on electricity, Mrs. Johnson cooks meals outdoors and Willie goes to bed at sundown.

Books at the local high school cost $28 a year. Recently Willie's oldest boy dropped out of school so that the younger one could stay. The boy wants to be a mechanic. His oldest sister wants to teach. Neither knows if they will make it. Willie wants to work again. But he has become so discouraged seeking work he hardly looks anymore.[1]

Appalachia, where Willie Johnson lives, covers parts of ten states stretching between Pittsburgh, Pennsylvania, and Birmingham, Alabama. It has been called the nation's major depressed area, for unemployment in Appalachia is almost one-half again above the national average, and wages for the working are 20 percent below average. The main industries in Appalachia, mining, agriculture, and lumber, employ fewer and fewer people each year. During the 1950's, 1.5 million fled from Appalachia. Of the 15 million remaining, almost half are suffering economically. Running water is a rarity in many parts of Appalachia; refrigerators and stoves are owned by so few families they have become a status symbol. The schools are inferior, and most inhabitants have not completed more than two years of high school. Appalachia, like the Tennessee River Valley in the 1920's, lags far behind the rest of the country.

The Faces of Poverty: 2. Homer Burleigh—Hillbilly in Chicago

Homer Burleigh left the hills of Alabama after fighting with his stepmother. He found a job in Detroit at $100 a week, bought a new car, and saved $3 thousand. He returned to Alabama with the money and ran through it in 10 months. Homer then settled down, married an Alabama girl, and brought her to Chicago. Seven years and five children later the factory where Homer worked started going on short time and Homer found another job. But he soon was in trouble because this plant, too, worked short hours and Homer was unable to continue supporting a family of seven on $300 a month while making monthly payments of $60 on his 1954 Pontiac. The finance company attached his salary, whereupon Homer changed his social security number and drew his wages under another name. Then his troubles grew worse. He developed running sores under his arms and the doctor ordered him to stop working. Homer therefore applied for welfare, but continued work during the two week period it usually takes to process welfare applications. When the city agency found Homer still working they denied his application on the grounds of fraud. The finance company then seized his car and his landlord gave him an eviction notice.[2]

The Faces of Poverty: 3. The Martins—Southern Negroes in Chicago

Little Harry Martin, age six, was born in Chicago, Illinois shortly after his father migrated from McCory, Arkansas. The plaster in the Martin's apartment is falling off the walls, the kitchen is made dark and dingy by the family laundry. The kitchen table has but three legs, and there aren't enough chairs in the house to allow all the children to sit down at one time for a meal. The toilet is out of order because the water pipe leading into it has frozen and burst. Harry and his six brothers and sisters sleep in one room in two beds; neither bed has a mattress.

Harry's father used to work in a meat packing plant in the neighborhood, but the plant moved away and the Martins have been on welfare ever since. During the winter the youngest Martin, who had been sleeping in a supermarket carriage, died of pneumonia. Harry's father started drinking and has not really been sober since.

Harry wants to be a lawyer when he grows up; a sister wants to be a nurse, and an older brother a doctor. But the Martins are Negroes, they live in the worst section of Chicago, they are supported by welfare, they go to inferior, overcrowded schools, and the father is now a drunkard. The children will probably learn that poor Negroes don't usually become doctors or lawyers.[3]

Migrants in the Slums

Both the Burleighs and the Martins are migrants; they, like 27 million other Americans, have flocked to the city in the past 40 years. They have fled farms like Willie Preston Canty's in South Carolina (Chapter 18) or homes like Willie Johnson's in Appalachia. They left poverty behind them and met it again in the city. In New York City, poverty is living in Harlem or the Bedford-Stuyvesant section of Brooklyn; in Chicago, poverty is West Garfield Park; in Los Angeles, it is Watts. By the end of the 1950's more people lived in city slums of this type than lived on farms. Here, in the hearts of our great cities, the unemployment rate runs up to 30 percent (as in Watts); over 1,200,000 in New York alone qualify for public assistance; up to three times more children die in infancy than in the better districts; and over 100 thousand in New York City are juvenile delinquents, or live "on the verge of the underworld, shuttling between it and the rest of society."[4]

For the Burleighs and the Martins, the American dream is shattered in the reality of broken glass, dilapidated buildings, overcrowded tenements, and the smells of poverty. For Willie Preston Canty, the dream is staying on his farm and avoiding the misery of the city.

The Faces of Poverty: 4. Edmund MacIntosh and the Golden Years

For Edmund MacIntosh, the American dream, a fragile hope in youth, has become an empty illusion at age 76. MacIntosh lives in Los Angeles on his Social Security, which amounts to about $600 a year. He pays $38.50 for a lonely room and spends $12.50 each month for food and chewing tobacco. Since his illness prevents him from leaving his rooming house, he has friends buy him dry cereal, two cans of Spam, several cans of vegetable juice, and two dozen eggs each week. Ed boils the eggs immediately since he has no refrigerator, and he just hopes the meat won't spoil. Sometimes it does.

Edmund MacIntosh fought in World Wars I and II. Between the wars he owned a newspaper stand on Times Square, New York, and was put out of business by the Depression. By the time the Depression ended, he was making $3 thousand a year in the newspaper distribution business in Washington, D.C. Ed was married and had a daughter. When World War II came, Ed enlisted at the age of 52. His wife left him while he was overseas.

Returning from World War II, Ed MacIntosh found an $80 a week job as a railroad guard in California and worked until he was laid off. He supported himself for several years mowing lawns in the Los Angeles area, but power mowers cut into his business and Ed, then two years over retirement age, collected $1250 in back Social Security and started living on his $50 monthly pension. Doctor bills and other unexpected expenses have decreased his savings to $250.[5]

Edmund MacIntosh's case is all too typical of our senior citizens. In what might have been their "golden years," 8 million, which is half the population over 60, are poor. In 1959, the average monthly income from Social Security was only $70; more than half had saved less than $1 thousand and contributions from their children amounted to less than 10 percent of their incomes.

Like Edmund MacIntosh, most of the aged are lonely. One-third don't have phones, a good number are sick, and many (until the recent passage of the Medicare Bill) could not afford to pay their doctor bills. In 1892, when MacIntosh was born, 70 percent of the aged worked; today only one out of five works. The rest generally have not managed to save enough to lead a graceful and secure life in retirement. Society doesn't allow them to work, the young reject them, age claims its toll in illness, and retirement doesn't afford them a decent standard of living.

The War on Poverty

On November 19, 1963, President John Kennedy, well informed on the facts of poverty, decided his administration would accept the challenge of putting an end to it. He relayed this decision to his chief economic advisor. Three days later, the President was dead. But his successor, Lyndon Johnson, proclaimed the fight against poverty as "my kind of program" and decided to move "full speed ahead."[6] Congress cooperated and passed the Economic Opportunity Act, allocating nearly $1 billion. President Johnson chose Sargeant Shriver to head the campaign. With Shriver installed in the Office of Economic Opportunity, the new Federal agency began its multiphase program. The next year (1965), Congress increased its original allotment to $1.8 billion. The money was divided among a bewildering number of projects. They included:

$667 million to Community Action programs—by far the largest single outlay and the most controversial aspect of the anti-poverty war. Community action programs aim to coordinate activities of existing private and public agencies designed to help the poor. They try giving the poor an opportunity to participate in formulating the programs designed to help them, under the assumption that the poor (more than the social workers) know what is needed most. In the process, Community Action attempts to avoid the controls over welfare programs traditionally exercised by politicians in city halls and state capitols. In some cases, federal aid has been used to organize rent strikes, voter registration campaigns, and other protests which have embarrassed local politicians. These politicians have tried ending Community Action programs or at least rechanneling them to more conventional activities: fencing classes, health centers, and day camps. The battles over Community Action programs are further complicated by the fear, real or imagined, that irresponsible or corrupt leaders are gaining control over these activities. With $667 million riding on the revolutionary issue of the poor controlling their own destiny, the stakes are high for city hall politicians and the poor's genuine leaders.

$150 million to Operation Head Start—designed to give pre-school children (4–6) a chance to make up for the lack of educational opportunities at home. In the summer of 1965, Head Start gave an 8-week enrichment program to over a half-million young; plans for 1966 call for pre-kindergarten classes and a million or more in summer classes.

$281 million for the Job Corps—to train high school dropouts, age 16–21, for full time jobs. Trainees are sent to camps, away from city or country slums; they are paid a small monthly wage, and they are trained in skills which will help them find work upon graduation.

$300 million for the Neighborhood Youth Corps—to employ needy teenagers in maintaining parks, painting signs, doing clerical work, etc.

Other programs, generally costing under $100 million, include a domestic corps known as VISTA (Volunteers in Service to America), a small loans program for poor farmers and small businessmen, employment to help poor college students finance their educations, an adult education program, and an employment agency for adults.

Poverty Warriors Attack the Cycle of Poverty

Every campaign strategy is based on certain assumptions. President Johnson's strategy against poverty assumed that the poor were trapped in a vicious cycle:

> Poverty breeds poverty. A poor individual or family has a high probability of staying poor. Low incomes carry with them high risks of illness; limitations on mobility; limited access to education, information and training. Poor parents cannot give their children the opportunities for better health and education needed to improve their lot. Lack of motivation, hope, and incentive is a more subtle but no less powerful barrier than lack of financial means. Thus the cruel legacy of poverty is passed from parents to children.[7]

Break the cycle of poverty, the argument goes, and the poor are freed to participate in the richness of American life. On these grounds the administration placed its major emphasis on training and educating the poor.

Poverty War Aimed at the Poor, Not at Poverty?

Johnson's critics challenged his assumptions. Poverty, they argued, was inevitable as long as there were not enough jobs to go around or too many jobs that paid too little; besides, because of age, family responsibilities, or illness, many were unable to work. So long as the lack of employment opportunities persisted, would not training and education for the poor result only in a new class of well educated and well trained poverty-stricken people? These critics opposed the war on poverty on the assumption that it was directed against the poor and not against poverty itself. Unless the necessary jobs were somehow created, poverty would be eliminated only if the poor were given more money or cheaper services:

> Mr. Johnson's approach is, then, fundamentally conservative. It assumes that the poor are poor not because the economy is mismanaged but because the poor themselves have something wrong with them. They live in the wrong place and won't move. They have the wrong skills—or no skills at all—and won't enroll in training programs. They have too little education and won't go back to school. They have the wrong personality traits or bad health. They are too profligate [wasteful] to save when their earning power is high, and so have nothing left to supplement their inadequate relief or Social Security benefits. . . .

> What has been launched therefore is not just a war on poverty but a war on the poor, aiming to change them beyond all recognition. The aim is not just to provide them with a lower-middle class standard of living, but also with the lower-middle class virtues, such as they are. Out of $962 million (asked for in 1964), $887 million is to be spent on education, training, and character building.[8]

The solution, argued the critics, would not come from changing the poor by retraining them, but from supplementing their incomes through one or two basic methods:

1. Giving more money directly to the poor.
2. Giving them free goods and services.

Neither technique was revolutionary, for both had been introduced during the 1930's. While welfare payments supplemented the incomes of the poor, the WPA also employed many. Thus they were granted direct payments. Quadrupling Social Security payments and giving every poor family an income of $60 a week through a "negative" income tax would update this strategy. A new WPA could provide jobs for [help] the unemployed, who would be trained to provide the missing social services in our cities and to build needed houses, schools, and recreation facilities. Or, the United States could adopt a startling new plan which has worked successfully in Canada for 20 years: paying every family a "baby bonus" of $6 to $8 per child per month, granting the family at least enough money to feed, to clothe, and, perhaps, to educate the child. But the basic thing, according to critics who argued that low income was the key question, was a sure regular income; poverty could be eliminated with a stroke of the pen by simply channeling enough money or other aid directly to the poor at a cost of $10 to $15 billion a year.

Conservatives Criticize the "Cycle of Poverty Theory"

Critics in the 1960's, much like those of the 1930's, rejected any massive government program designed to alleviate poverty. They ridiculed th "cycle of poverty" theory put forward by President Johnson:

We are told, however, that many people lack skills and cannot find jobs be-cause they did not have an education. That's like saying that people have big feet because they wear big shoes. The fact is that most people who have no skill, have had no education for the same reason—low intelligence or low ambition.[9]

Arguing from the above assumption, and believing that welfare pro-grams were detrimental to incentive and socialistic in their consequences, these critics opposed Johnson's poverty program. Russell Bastley, public relations director of the Illinois Manufacturers' Association, explained the opposition to the Economic Opportunity Act of 1964 as follows:

. . . Our association believes the Economic Opportunity Act of 1964, mas-querading under the high-sounding name of a "war on poverty," is an imprac-tical, costly, highly dangerous political scheme to force through Congress many old, discredited programs and several new extreme plans for a welfare state.

If enacted, this new "dole" would:

Open the floodgates of unrestricted federal spending which could run as high as $15 billion per year.

Create a huge, new federal bureaucracy and add thousands of new politi-cal patronage jobs to the burgeoning federal payroll.

Regiment hundreds of thousands of Americans under a new government overseer.

Expand federal interference further into the fields of education, agricul-ture, and business.

And lead to more deficit spending and cheapening of the dollar, thereby making the so-called poor poorer than ever.

The American public is already being taxed at the rate of $44 billion a year to support welfare-type plans including relief, pensions, health-care programs, veterans' benefits, vocational training, *et cetera*.

This new scheme would add approximately another billion dollars in 1965 and would hand a new government agency a blank check thereafter.[10]

Summary and Problem

Even without massive federal programs to eliminate poverty, there had been a decline in the extent of poverty. As officially defined (an income of approximately $3 thousand for a family of four) poverty decreased from one out of two families in 1936 to approximately one out of three in 1947, one out of five in 1963, and one out of six in 1965 (though the rate of de-cline slipped between 1957 and 1963). Is this a satisfactory rate of progress in diminishing poverty? Are the critics correct in believing that the poor are largely to blame for their own condition and that government welfare programs are more dangerous than helpful? If so, the war on poverty should be canceled. But if one accepts President Johnson's "cycle of poverty" analysis, one must also accept his method of attacking the prob-lem by retraining the poor. And if won over by the argument that the system rather than the people needs changing, one must consider implementation of a new program of more direct welfare assistance and increased financial help for the poor, regardless of costs.

A fourth method of attacking poverty is to improve the general performance of the economy. This will be considered in the next chapter.

NOTES

1. Ben H. Badikian, "The Invisible American," *Saturday Evening Post,* December 21–28, 1963, pp. 28–31.

2. *Ibid.,* p. 37.

3. *Ibid.,* pp. 37–38.

4. Michael Harrington, *The Other America* (Baltimore: Penguin Books, 1962), p. 142.

5. Badikian, *op. cit.,* p. 33.

6. "Shriver and the War on Poverty," *Newsweek,* September 13, 1965, p. 22.

7. *Economic Report of the President,* transmitted to Congress January, 1964 (Washington, D.C.: U.S. Government Printing Office, 1964), pp. 69–70.

8. Christopher Jenks, "Johnson *vs.* Poverty." Reprinted by permission of *The New Republic,* © 1964, Harrison-Blaine of New Jersey, Inc.

9. *New York Times,* January 16, 1964, p. 21.

10. United States Congress, House of Representatives, Committee on Education and Labor, *Economic Opportunity Act of 1964,* hearings before Subcommittee on Poverty Program, 88th Congress, 1st Session, on H.R. 10440, Part III, April 22-28, 1964 (Washington, D.C.: U.S. Government Printing Office, 1964), p. 1299.

QUESTIONS

1. Do you think people like the Cantys, Burleighs, Martins, or MacIntoshes could escape poverty on their own initiative or do they need help? Explain.

2. Should the federal government help families like the above escape from poverty?

3. Assuming it is the federal government's responsibility to end poverty, how would this best be accomplished?

SUGGESTED READING

The recent rediscovery of poverty has produced a score of books on the subject. Ben H. Badikian renders a sensitive portrait of several people who are poor in *In the Midst of Plenty: A New Report on the Poor in America* (New York: New American Library, 1964). For a collection of readings aimed at the high school student see Gerald Leinwand (ed.), *Poverty and the Poor* (New York: Washington Square Press, 1968). A more analytic treatment is Leo Fishman (ed.), *Poverty and Affluence* (New Haven: Yale University Press, 1966), and Herman Miller (ed.), *Poverty, American Style* (Belmont, Calif.: Wadsworth Publishing Company, 1966). For contrasts of poverty and wealth see Herman Miller, *Rich Man, Poor Man* (New York: Thomas Y. Crowell, 1964). A general attack on helping the poor and interfering with economic laws is launched by Clarence B. Carson, *The War on the Poor* (New Rochelle, N.Y.: Arlington House, 1969).

Chapter 20
Taxes and Deficits

Introduction

When President Hoover tried to increase taxes and cut government expenses in 1932, he was working on the theory that increased private spending and balanced budgets would restore confidence, and with confidence would come recovery. When Roosevelt reduced WPA rolls in 1937, he hoped business recovery would more than make up for the slack left by diminished government employment. Both presidents, understandably, sought to balance the budget by increases in taxes and by reductions in federal expenditures. Both presidents believed budget balancing improves the economy.

Many years later, in 1954 and again in 1957, President Dwight Eisenhower reduced federal taxes. When a business slump caused a mild recession in 1958, Eisenhower ordered an emergency increase in spending amounting to nearly $7 billion. As soon as the recession was under control, the President worked to get the budget back into balance.

In January, 1963, President Kennedy recommended a cut in taxes which eventually amounted to $11.5 billion. This tax cut put the federal government in the red by $12 billion and increased the total federal debt to $310 billion. Congress approved this tax cut in February, 1964. At that time no business recession was threatening the country; wages and employment had soared to record heights. Nor did the President or Congress recommend a decrease in federal spending to offset reduced federal income. This action became the first time in American history that president and Congress courted budget deficits during prosperity to bolster the economy. Predictably, Kennedy's proposal was opposed by champions of the balanced budget. But it was simultaneously criticized by advocates of increased federal spending who would rather create deficits by raising expenditures than by lowering taxes. America's economic leaders had

170

come to reject the philosophy of the balanced budget and to accept Keynes' theory of stimulating economic growth through federal deficits. This chapter studies the 1964 tax cut that signaled acceptance of Keynes and traces the bitter arguments over cutting taxes. The chapter will help the reader decide whether tax cuts and/or increased spending, or balanced budgets, bring prosperity.

Inadequate Growth One Reason for the Tax Cut

The reasons for the tax cut were summarized by President Kennedy on March 11, 1963:

> Unemployment is our number one economic problem. It wastes the lives of men and women, depriving both them and the Nation. Our continued under-use of human and physical capacity is costing us some $30 to $40 billion of additional goods and services annually. This means a considerably lower standard of living than we would otherwise enjoy. More seriously—ominously —it means we are doing less than our best in staffing ourselves in the struggle for freedom at home and abroad that now commands our energies and re-sources on an unprecedented scale, and in ever more demanding forms. [1]

President Kennedy might have added that our economy was growing at a rate of 2.5 percent, less rapidly than the economy of any other major country; that the Russians with a 6 percent growth rate actually believed they could overtake us by 1980; and that over 6 percent of all Americans were without jobs and that an average of 5.5 percent had been out of work during the past six years. Every day the value of the goods and services the unemployed workers were not producing totaled $100 million, costing the government many millions in taxes. The money needed to end poverty, to provide needed services like schools, and to assist undeveloped regions like Appalachia could come from employing this idle manpower.

Kennedy to Rely on the Multiplier

Kennedy assumed the tax cut would increase the rate of economic growth to the point of increasing taxable income and ultimately enabling the government to collect more taxes. The $11.5 billion tax cut would provide a stimulus to spending. Consumers would have more money to spend on cars, refrigerators, clothes, and the like, which in turn would result in increased output, in more employment, and again in more spending. Businessmen would invest some of the money they did not have to pay in taxes, to expand their plants and hire more workers. The combined effect of increased consumption and business investment should multiply the $11.5 billion tax cut into $25 to $35 billion of economic expansion. This larger taxable base supposedly would yield more tax revenues than would be collected while higher tax rates were in effect.

As has been explained in Chapter 10, a British economist, John Maynard Keynes, first developed the reasoning behind the investment and consumption multiplier. But it was not until the 1960's that any American president fully believed in it. Below, Kennedy's chief economic advisor, Walter Heller, explains the multiplier to the Senate Finance Committee:

The way in which an $11 billion tax reduction would translate itself into an increase of some $30 billion in total demand is increasingly well understood. After-tax consumer incomes would rise, at existing levels of production, by some $8.8 billion from individual tax reduction, and by an additional $1 billion from corporate tax [reduction through higher dividends]. As consumer after-tax incomes rise, their spending on the purchase of consumer goods and services also rises. In fact, during each of the past dozen years, consumers in the aggregate have spent close to 93 percent of their available after-tax incomes on purchases of current output, and they would soon adjust their spending to restore that rate. To meet this added demand, some $9 billion of extra annual production of consumer goods and services would be generated. The production of these extra goods and services—using labor now unwillingly idle and plants now insufficiently utilized—would generate new payrolls, profits, and farm and professional incomes. This extra income in turn would be respent on added goods and services, generating repeated further cycles of income and spending, for a total direct comsumption impact of more than $18 billion a year.

At the same time, incentives to invest would be strengthened, both by reduction of business taxes and by the fuller use of existing plant and equipment. Extra business investment, together with higher residential construction and increased state and local government spending—financed by higher state and local tax yields from an expanding tax base—could add another $5 to $7 billion of annual demand and production. This production, too, would raise incomes, reinforcing consumer spending by another $5 to $7 billion. An expansion in production of approximately $30 billion per year (at this year's level of gross national product and income) is thus a reasonable expectation based on economic experience. . . . [2]

Keyserling Criticizes the Tax Cut

Not everyone agreed with the Kennedy administration that reducing taxes was the best method of stimulating growth. Among the administration's most active and intelligent critics was Leon Keyserling, the former chief economic advisor to President Harry Truman; who voiced two major objections to the tax cut:

1. He objected to increasing businessmen's profits; he thought excess plant capacity, not low profits, was hindering business expansion.

2. He believed the administration's bill unnecessarily favored wealthy at the expense of poor taxpayers.

The effects of a tax cut favoring wealthy corporations and families, Keyserling argued, are far less stimulating to the economy than a corresponding increase in government expenditures. Therefore, while Keyserling agreed with the President that a deficit would stimulate the economy, he preferred to create this deficit by increasing federal spending rather than decreasing taxes. Finally, and perhaps most important, increased federal spending could directly benefit the poor, who were too impoverished to be helped by a tax cut.

The 1964 tax cut reduced corporation or business taxes by $2.4 billion dollars. This reduction came on the heels of a $2 billion tax concession granted businessmen in 1962. The two cuts on business taxes promised to increase corporation after-tax income by 35 percent. At a time when businessmen were operating at 15 percent less than full capacity, Keyserling argued, this concession would tend only to encourage the introduction of labor-saving machinery and replace rather than employ more workers:

> *Mr. Keyserling:* Now, when corporate profits are higher than ever before, when retained earnings are higher than ever before, when the Secretary of the Treasury and many others have admitted that we have a prolixity of savings jammed up in all of our savings institutions, when we have large unused plant capacity, why do we need to pay out about $4 billion in subsidies involved in this corporate tax cut plus the cut of 1962 to increase the after-tax disposable income of investors by 35 percent? What are they going to do with the money?
>
> They are going to save much of it. Much of this tax cut is going to be wasted. . . . ³
>
> The trouble is not with the profit-sales ratios; the trouble is with the volume of sales. In other words, if plants are operating with 15 percent idle capacity, which is the typical experience now, the right way to increase their profits is to create a condition in the American economy where they will be operating at 90 percent or 92 percent of capacity, not to give them a tax bonanza so that the ratio of their per unit after-tax profits will be even higher than now, although they are breaking all records now.
>
> That is what this bill would do. . . .
>
> *Senator Ribicoff:* In the sense of what you are saying, if they have this excess capacity, while they may have a year or two more profits, there will be another dip. . . .⁴

Keyserling also opposed reducing taxes because he thought taxes were being cut at the wrong end of the income scales. The tax cut, the economist figured, would save the family earning $200 thousand a year 16 percent of their income and the family earning $3 thousand a year a mere 2 percent. Since the rich save more of their income than the poor, much of the tax cut would be saved and not spent, thereby diminishing the effect of the multiplier and increasing already swollen savings.

> The way I figure it, . . . about $4 billion of those personal tax cuts would go to families with incomes over $10 thousand. That does not sound very high, but they are only 12.5 percent of all taxpayers. Only 55 percent would go to taxpayers with incomes under $10 thousand, who are about 87.5 percent of all taxpayers. A substantial part of the tax cuts going to the top 12.5 percent would, for reasons I have given, be saved for the purposes of investment, and therefore would be substantially wasted. . . .
>
> The $3 thousand family would have a 2 percent increase in its disposable income under this bill. The $200 thousand family would have a 16 percent increase in its disposable income.
>
> To state it simply, the more income you have now before taxes the bigger increase in disposable income you will get under the bill. . . .⁵

Since much of the reduced taxes would increase savings, Keyserling concluded, cutting taxes is a less effective economic stimulant than increasing expenditures. Furthermore, tax cuts would not help those with little or no income (like the poor of depressed Appalachia); nor would they provide unfulfilled public needs such as more schools or public works:

> *Mr. Keyserling:* I would say this—I think I have said it—first of all, the $11 billion tax cut, if it had a multiplier of three, would give you $33 billion of increased stimulation.

> As I developed rather fully in my testimony, the wastage that would come from this tax bill, I figure a wastage in the range of 25 percent, would reduce that $33 billion by a quarter, roughly speaking, which is about $8 billion to $9 billion, so let's say reduce the $33 billion to $24 billion in terms of stimulus.

> Now, I do not want to get into that too much, because I believe in consumer tastes and choices, but nonetheless, I do believe that, with the great gaps we have in our public needs, they have a high order of priority quite aside from the quantitative stimulus. . . .

> *Senator Gore:* . . . One other point, though. One other point. Suppose that there is an area in America, for example the Appalachian, where, because of automation in the coal mines, because of various economic factors, there is a very high rate of unemployment.

> Suppose that you have a problem in West Virginia such as was discovered in the last [election] campaign. Now, how does a general tax reduction reach an Appalachian Mountain village?

> *Mr. Keyserling:* It would take as long as it is taking me to try to convince some people in the administration that they ought to re-examine their ideas in the light of actualities.[7]

Eisenhower Opposes Reducing Taxes
Without Cutting Expenditures

While Keyserling opposed tax reduction without *increasing* government spending, President Eisenhower would not cut taxes without first *reducing* government spending. In an open letter addressed to Republican Congressional leaders in October, 1963, the former president urged a $10 to $15 billion reduction in spending in order to balance the budget. In an article appearing in the *Saturday Evening Post,* Eisenhower explained his reasons:
1. Recent budget deficits make balancing the budget an absolute necessity, for a government, like a family, cannot long afford to live beyond its means.
2. Economic growth, though necessary, should not be forced by federal action to fill a certain prescribed percentage each year.
Based on these assumptions, Eisenhower's conclusion followed logically; balance the budget first and only then can you afford to cut taxes or increase government spending.
Under President Kennedy's tax program, the federal deficit in 1964 and 1965 would run approximately $20 billion with no balanced budget in

sight over the years ahead. These debts Eisenhower felt were obligations which future generations must pay. A government, like an individual, Eisenhower argued, must live within its means if it is to avoid ruin.

I have no desire to be an alarmist. However, the time has come when my sense of duty as a citizen demands that I speak out bluntly regarding what I believe to be a clear danger which could threaten our free way of life and our security as a nation. That threat is the determined effort of our current political leaders to commit the United States to a risky, highly experimental fiscal adventure, based on a questionable theory which I shall call "spending for spending's sake." That policy, which fails to heed the plain lessons of history, now has been unveiled in what I consider a vast, reckless scope, calling for a larger-than-wartime budget, a deep tax cut and a deliberate plunge into a massive deficit. Let us review the principal figures briefly: a budget of $98.8 billion, . . . a tax cut estimated to reach over $10 billion a year by 1965; and an estimated deficit of $11.9 billion for fiscal 1964—on top of a current one of $8.8 billion with further "planned" deficits extending into 1967, if not longer. . .

. . . No party doctrine is necessary to tell us that if the present generation keeps passing its bills to the next one, our children and grandchildren will inherit not a free country, bright with opportunity, but a vast wasteland of debt and financial chaos. . . .

The federal government's financial affairs are immense and complex, but their sound management is not a mysterious art; in fact, they are subject to the same time-tested rules as those followed by any farsighted householder or businessman. A wise family or a well-run enterprise makes a practice of spending less than it takes in; in good years the family builds up savings for its future needs, for sending the youngsters to college, for meeting possible emergencies such as ill health, or unemployment; a business builds up reserves for carrying itself safely over poor years and for expansion and investment in new opportunities. . . .

I say that *the time-tested rules of financial policy still apply. Spending for spending's sake is patently a false theory. No family, no business, no nation can spend itself into prosperity.* [8]

Of course, the country must have economic growth, but when so-called experts say that it must be a certain number of percentage points per year, I just think they don't know what they are talking about. It's like saying that each and every child should grow the same number of inches a year. And when they say that government spending should be the controlling factor in expansion, I regard this as a pernicious myth. [9]

Cutting spending, Eisenhower argued, takes courage, but the budget can be trimmed without reducing any essential federal expenditure. Then lower taxes can stimulate economic growth and surplus revenues can start debt retirement and increase government service.

. . . And as a precondition to any reduction in taxes we must have the courage to cut spending. I still insist that the proposed budget is extravagant and can be cut by billions of dollars without harming a single *essential* federal function.

The government formula now given us is: Spend more, collect less, go more in debt. Doesn't this whole proposition put the cart before the horse? If we reduce public spending *and* taxes at the same time, then our economy will have its best opportunity for showing new growth. When we reach that happy stage where, with lower tax rates, the budget shows a surplus, *then* we can see our way clear to pay off a bit of our debt and devote more money to government services for an expanding population.[10]

The Tax Cut—A Historic Measure

Congress rejected both Eisenhower's and Keyserling's advice, and after considering the tax proposal for 13 months, passed the measure. In February, 1964, President Johnson signed the history-making bill into law:

WASHINGTON, Feb. 26—A stroke of President Johnson's pen today started the nation on what is probably the most important innovation and experiment in its economic history.

With the enactment of the $11.5 billion tax cut, after 13 months of debate and doubt, the United States has been firmly set on the road of economics developed nearly 30 years ago by the British economist John Maynard Keynes.[11]

In September, 1966, President Johnson asked Congress to raise the same business taxes to slow economic expansion that President Kennedy had reduced to stimulate growth. The need for this dramatic reversal is in itself significant. The 1964 tax cut had been in effect for only two years, but the situation had changed. The great economic problems were no longer slow growth, unemployment, or unused plant capacity, but rapid, inflationary expansion, and occasional critical shortages of skilled labor, resources, and plant capacity. Perhaps the tax cut had been too successful. Perhaps the increased spending due to the war in Vietnam had created these shortages.

President Johnson could also have fought inflation by reducing government spending. Certainly, his conservative critics called on him to pursue this course. But Johnson was also responding to criticism from liberals who claimed the War on Poverty and other "Great Society" programs were suffering from lack of funds. The taxation and spending choices open to the President have already been thoroughly discussed in this chapter. Each Congress and each President must decide anew how best to use these fiscal tools to affect economic growth. The economic well-being of the American people depends on how intelligently these choices are made.

Congress was willing to make the experiment of cutting taxes to stimulate growth. The results of the experiment can be read on any given day in current magazines and newspapers, which frequently report on America's economic conditions. Sketched out in the charts below is a brief summary graph of the economy's course before and after the tax cut. Notice, particularly, the changes in unemployment and in GNP (Gross National Product). Supplement these observations with more current statistics. Does this evidence indicate the accuracy of Kennedy's, Keyserling's, or Eisenhower's forecasts? On the basis of the evidence and the arguments, are more tax cuts, increased federal spending, or budget balancing desirable?

Wholesale Prices

Wholesale prices rose fractionally in August. Price declines of 1.4% in farm products and 0.4% in processed foods and feeds were more than offset by a rise of 0.4% in industrial commodity prices.

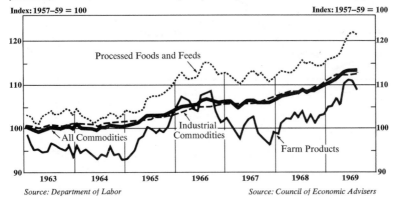

Index: 1957–59 = 100   Index: 1957–59 = 100

Source: Department of Labor   Source: Council of Economic Advisers

Index: 1957–59 = 100

	All commodities	Farm products	Processed foods and feeds	Industrial commodities					
				All industrials	Crude materials	Intermediate materials	Producer finished goods	Consumer finished goods excluding food	
								Durable	Nondurable
1959	100.6	97.2	99.9	101.3	102.3	101.0	102.1	101.3	100.8
1960	100.7	96.9	100.0	101.3	98.3	101.4	102.3	100.9	101.5
1961	100.3	96.0	101.6	100.8	97.2	100.1	102.5	100.5	101.5
1962	100.6	97.7	102.7	100.8	95.6	99.9	102.9	100.0	101.6
1963	100.3	95.7	103.3	100.7	94.3	99.6	103.1	99.5	101.9
1964	100.5	94.3	103.1	101.2	97.1	100.2	104.1	99.9	101.6
1965	102.5	98.4	106.7	102.5	100.9	101.5	105.4	99.6	102.8
1966	105.9	105.6	113.0	104.7	104.5	103.6	108.0	100.2	104.8
1967	106.1	99.7	111.7	106.3	100.0	104.8	111.5	101.7	107.2
1968	108.7	102.2	114.1	109.0	101.8	107.5	115.3	103.9	109.4
1968: Jul	109.1	103.9	115.9	108.8	100.9	107.3	115.2	103.3	110.0
Aug . . .	108.7	101.4	114.9	108.9	101.0	107.4	115.4	103.6	109.7
Sep. . . .	109.1	102.8	115.3	109.2	101.5	107.8	115.7	103.4	109.9
Oct. . . .	109.1	101.2	114.4	109.7	102.2	108.1	116.4	104.9	110.0
Nov . . .	109.6	103.1	114.7	109.9	103.0	108.2	116.9	105.0	110.2
Dec . . .	109.8	103.3	114.7	110.2	103.8	108.8	117.1	105.0	110.2
1969: Jan	110.7	104.9	116.0	110.9	105.0	109.7	117.6	105.1	110.4
Feb. . . .	111.1	105.0	116.3	111.4	105.5	110.4	117.8	105.1	110.7
Mar . . .	111.7	106.5	116.4	112.0	107.2	111.1	118.0	105.3	111.2
Apr . . .	111.9	105.6	117.3	112.1	109.0	111.0	118.1	105.4	111.5
May . . .	112.8	110.5	119.4	112.2	109.7	111.1	118.5	105.4	111.4
Jun. . . .	113.2	111.2	121.4	112.2	110.2	110.8	118.7	105.5	112.2
Jul	113.3	110.5	122.0	112.4	110.7	110.9	119.3	105.6	112.6
Aug . . .	113.4	108.9	121.5	112.8	112.5	111.3	119.3	105.2	113.0

Source: Department of Labor.

Federal Debt as a Percentage of Gross National Product

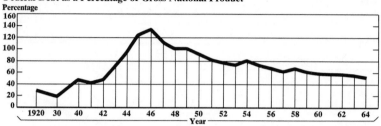

Source: Otto Eckstein, Public Finance

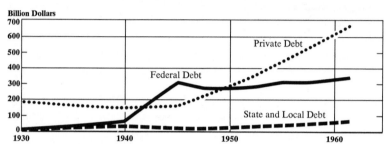

Source: Otto Eckstein, Public Finance

Employment, Unemployment, and Wages
Status of the Labor Force

The civilian labor force (seasonally adjusted) rose by 298,000 in August.
Employment rose by 313,000 and unemployment declined by 15,000

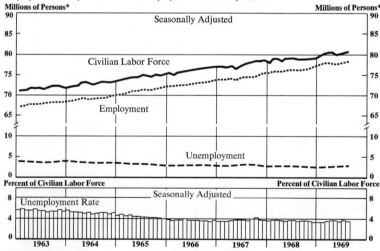

16 years of age and over.
Source: Department of Labor   Source: Council of Economic Advisers

Thousands of persons 16 years of age and over

	Total labor force (including armed forces)	Civilian employment (Unadjusted)		Unemployment	Total labor force (including armed forces)	Civilian labor force	Civilian employment (Seasonally adjusted)			Unemployment	Unemployment rate (percent of civilian labor force)		Labor force participation rate, unadjusted[1]
		Total	Non-agricultural				Total	Agricultural	Non-agricultural		Unadjusted	Seasonally adjusted	
											Percent		
1964	75,830	69,305	64,782	3786	75,830	73,091	69,305	4523	64,782	3786	5.2	......	59.6
1965	77,178	71,088	66,726	3366	77,178	74,455	71,088	4361	66,726	3366	4.5	......	59.7
1966	78,893	72,895	68,915	2875	78,893	75,770	72,895	3979	68,915	2875	3.8	......	60.1
1967	80,793	74,372	70,527	2975	80,793	77,347	74,372	3844	70,527	2975	3.8	......	60.6
1968	82,272	75,920	72,103	2817	82,272	78,737	75,920	3817	72,103	2817	3.6	......	60.7
1968: Jul	84,550	77,746	73,270	3217	82,504	78,917	76,020	3825	72,195	2897	4.0	3.7	62.3
Aug	83,792	77,432	73,325	2772	82,338	78,749	75,973	3751	72,222	2776	3.5	3.5	61.7
Sep	82,137	75,939	72,103	2606	82,438	78,847	76,000	3651	72,349	2847	3.3	3.6	60.4
Oct	82,477	76,364	72,596	2511	82,403	78,800	76,002	3525	72,477	2798	3.2	3.6	60.5
Nov	82,702	76,609	73,001	2577	82,559	79,042	76,388	3706	72,682	2654	3.3	3.4	60.6
Dec	82,618	76,700	73,421	2419	82,868	79,368	76,765	3842	72,923	2603	3.1	3.3	60.5
1969: Jan	81,711	75,358	72,192	2876	83,351	79,874	77,229	3752	73,477	2645	3.7	3.3	59.7
Feb	82,579	76,181	72,896	2923	83,831	80,356	77,729	3881	73,848	2627	3.7	3.3	60.3
Mar	82,770	76,520	73,193	2746	83,999	80,495	77,767	3732	74,035	2728	3.5	3.4	60.4
Apr	83,137	77,079	73,471	2542	83,966	80,450	77,605	3664	73,941	2845	3.2	3.5	60.5
May	83,085	77,264	73,370	2299	83,593	80,071	77,265	3805	73,460	2806	2.9	3.5	60.4
Jun	85,880	78,956	74,589	3400	83,957	80,433	77,671	3705	73,966	2762	4.1	3.4	62.4
Jul	86,318	79,616	75,460	3182	84,277	80,756	77,874	3551	74,323	2882	3.8	3.6	62.6
Aug	86,046	79,646	75,669	2869	84,584	81,054	78,187	3634	74,553	2867	3.5	3.5	62.3

[1] Total labor force as percent of noninstitutional population.

Note: Beginning 1960, data include Alaska and Hawaii.

Source: Department of Labor.

NOTES

1. "America the Backward," *The New Republic,* March 30, 1963, p. 3.

2. United States Congress, Senate, Committee on Finance, *Revenue Act of 1963,* 88th Congress, 1st Session, on H.R. 8363, Part IV, November 12–15, 1963 (Washington, D.C.: U.S. Government Printing Office, 1963), pp. 1582, 1583.

3. *Ibid.,* p. 689.

4. *Ibid.,* pp. 669–670.

5. *Ibid.,* p. 703.

6. *Ibid.,* pp. 704–705.

7. *Ibid.,* pp. 735–736.

8. Dwight D. Eisenhower, "Spending into Trouble," *Saturday Evening Post,* May 18, 1963, pp. 15–16.

9. *Ibid.,* p. 18.

10. *Ibid.*

11. *New York Times,* February 27, 1964, p. 18.

QUESTIONS

1. Summarize the fundamental reason for cutting taxes and pose counter arguments stated by Keyserling and Eisenhower.

2. Should a poor farmer in South Carolina or an unemployed miner in Appalachia favor cutting taxes? Would either benefit from a balanced budget? Explain your answers.

3. Do you agree with former President Eisenhower that governments, like individuals, must live within their incomes? Explain with specific reference to increased growth rates since 1964.

4. Based upon changes in economic growth and unemployment, was the tax cut a wise decision?

SUGGESTED READING

For a collection of articles considering fiscal and monetary policies to spur economic growth see Walter Heller (ed.), *Perspectives on Economic Growth* (New York: Random House, 1968). For an anti-spending view see Dwight D. Eisenhower, "Spending into Trouble," *Saturday Evening Post,* May 18, 1963. Sidney Ratner, *Taxation and Democracy in America,* 2nd ed. (New York: John Wiley and Sons, Inc., 1967) is a general survey. Since the economic problems of the 1970's are beginning to resemble those of the 1950's, the following books may be useful: Arthur M. Okun, *The Battle Against Unemployment: An Introduction to a Current Issue of Public Policy* (New York: W. W. Norton and Company, 1965), Edmund S. Phelps (ed.), *The Goals of Economic Growth: An Introduction to a Current Issue of Public Policy* (New York: W. W. Norton and Company, 1962), and Alvin H. Hansen, *Economic Issues of the 1960's* (New York: McGraw-Hill Book Co., 1960).

Index